praise for WHAT SHE'S NOT TELLING YOU

"This book exposes the serious consequences of 'literal listenin' and taking what women say at face value and teach᠁ ᠁ᵉ, not-so-simple thing: getting women to te᠁ ᠁ Woman women have nailed it."

—CHERYL CALLAN, SVP, Marketing

"The relationship between brands anc ᠁ ᠁nged forever and the quality of your dialogue with ᠁ direct proportion to how well you understand them. Mary Lou and her colleagues have exposed just how far we still have to go to get to the real truth inside women's heads. Ignore this insight at your peril."

—MARK BAYNES, Vice President, Global CMO, Kellogg Company

"Just Ask a Woman is in the forefront of understanding what really motivates women. You will listen more deeply, assess more easily, and engage more meaningfully for insights that lead to powerful marketplace results."

—DONNA STURGESS, Founding Partner, Buyology, Inc., and former Head of Innovation, GlaxoSmithKline

"Finally a marketing book that brings new meaning to the term retail therapy! This book puts marketers AND female consumers on the couch to teach how strategic interviewing and analysis can reveal profitable answers."

—NANCY BERK, PhD, clinical psychologist, researcher, humorist

"This book 'gets it'! A truly insightful tool that will help marketers better understand what women are really saying! This book is a must if you want to hear the Whole Truth and understand the 'GAMES' women play."

—REBECCA NOEL, Associate Director, Market Research, Kao Brands

"Healthcare professionals know that getting women to open up about what's really bothering them is the first step to healing. This marketing book brilliantly teaches how to get under women's skin!"

—ELLEN S. MARMUR, MD, Chief, Division of Dermatologic & Cosmetic Surgery, Department of Dermatology, Mount Sinai Medical Center

what she's not telling you

Why Women Hide
the Whole Truth
and What Marketers
Can Do About It

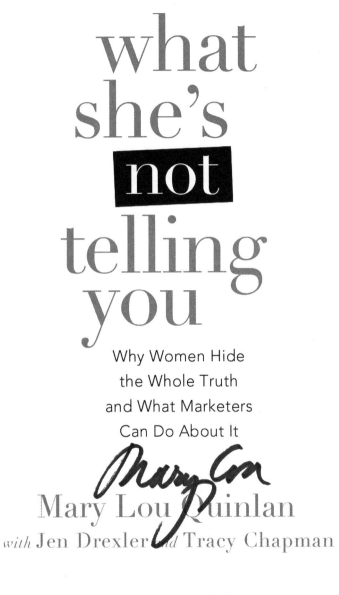

Mary Lou Quinlan

with Jen Drexler *and* Tracy Chapman

just ask a
woman

Published by Just Ask a Woman Media
New York, NY
www.justaskawoman.com

Distributed by Greenleaf Book Group LLC

For ordering information or special discounts for bulk purchases, please contact
Greenleaf Book Group LLC at PO Box 91869, Austin, TX 78709, 512.891.6100.

Design and composition by Greenleaf Book Group LLC
Cover design by Greenleaf Book Group LLC
Author photo: Stephanie Halmos
Stylist: Mordechai Alvow
Stock photography: Istockphoto

Publisher's Cataloging-In-Publication Data
(Prepared by The Donohue Group, Inc.)

Quinlan, Mary Lou.
   What she's not telling you : why women hide the whole truth and what marketers
can do about it / Mary Lou Quinlan with Jen Drexler and Tracy Chapman.
-- 1st ed.

   p. : ill. ; cm.

   ISBN: 978-0-9823938-0-2

1. Women consumers. 2. Consumer behavior. 3. Women--Attitudes.
4. Marketing. I. Drexler, Jen. II. Chapman, Tracy (Tracy Lee), 1973- III. Title.

HC79.C6 Q56 2010
658.80082   2009932968

Part of the Tree Neutral™ program, which offsets the number of
trees consumed in the production and printing of this book by
taking proactive steps, such as planting trees in direct proportion
to the number of trees used: www.treeneutral.com

Printed in the United States of America on acid-free paper

10 11 12 13 14   10 9 8 7 6 5 4 3 2

TO THE WOMEN WHO LED US
AND THE MEN WHO ARE BEHIND US

CONTENTS

the Whole Truth behind her Half Truth

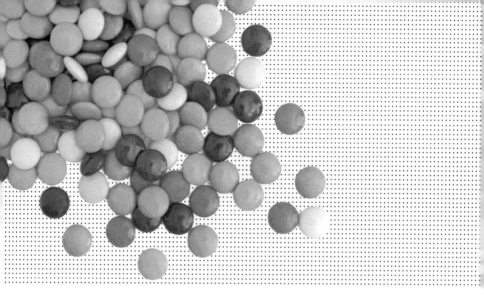

Y ou're in the dark—literally.

It's 11 a.m. but the dim lighting makes it feel like nighttime in a hushed room in a nondescript building off an interstate. You're feeling tense as you watch a group of women talk about your new product concepts on the other side of a one-way mirror. It's your third city in three days and you're feeling the pressure to be home, or back at the office, or anywhere but here in focus group hell. You're looking for any shred of hope that you've finally nailed the *big* idea but so far, they hate everything.

You glance furtively at your BlackBerry and munch Peanut M&M's and then continue grimly staring through the glass. Your plans are already over deadline and you can't send the agency back to the drawing board one more time. If this group doesn't like something soon, you're thinking of hurling the M&M's at them. These eight women you've never met are about to destroy your last good idea and you are fit to be tied.

The women, eerily aware of your surveillance, are listening to the last shot you've got. And suddenly one woman perks up. She likes it.

She really likes it. Then a second one chimes in. And another. You're feeling the love. You've got a potential blockbuster on your hands. At last. You can head back home with a win.

Eight months later . . .

Your new product is such a flop that the stores are pulling it off the shelves. Why did those women say they loved it when they didn't? Why did they tell you one thing and do another? Were they lying? Were you buying it? Why, why, why?

You're in the dark—literally.

what your best customers aren't telling you

Women are the most powerful customers on the planet, influencing or purchasing 85% of everything you make, sell, or offer.

They're the voices on your customer service line, the cash at your counter, and the fingertips on your website. Whether you're in consumer packaged goods, retail, service, technology, finance, health-care, or any category you can name, they're the "It Girls" of your marketing plan and the lifeblood of your sales and profits. Knowing what women want is your ticket to big ideas and big money.

Unfortunately, and this likely shocks or baffles you, women don't always say what they really mean, especially to the market-ers who want their money. So we're about to divulge what women aren't telling you. After a decade of listening to women as partners in our strategic marketing firm, Just Ask a Woman, we've detected a critical behavior among female consumers: the tendency to dis-close what we call Half Truths (what they are willing to admit) and to hide Whole Truths (what they really believe, do, and buy). These Half Truths, particularly the deadly five that we'll discuss in detail, can undermine your marketing results by encouraging you to throw good money after bad insights.

the Half Truth is what women are willing to admit.

the Whole Truth is what they really believe, do, and buy.

As a marketer, you've probably been a victim of her drive-by duplicity at some point. Have you ever heard a woman swear that she loves your new product and then watch her buy a competitor's product? Ever wonder why women claim your store is their favorite yet rarely visit it? Or have you ever rejoiced as women raved about your ads in research only to discover months and millions of lost dollars later that they've all changed their minds?

With little provocation, the average female respondent can dance her way through a game of mental dodgeball with billion dollar marketers. You may not want to believe that women are hiding the Whole Truth from your brand. But would you know it if they were?

her Half Truths will cost you

Buying into Half Truths will only get you halfway to your marketing goals: so-so strategies, unremarkable products, mediocre communications, and routine retail experiences. In other words, you may be leaving half the money on the table.

If you're trying to get her attention, her dollars, or her loyalty, you've got to avoid buying into the Half Truths that can undermine your best-laid plans. Only her Whole Truths can save you from a marketing mistake before it's millions of dollars too late.

Stop throwing good money after bad insights.

To help you solve this problem, we will be your truth detectors, your insiders in the Half Truth epidemic that you're paying for—not just in billions of wasted dollars in concept development, market research, and creative exploration, but in the marketplace, where it really hurts.

Just ask the leaders at **THE GAP** why they opened and quickly shuttered **FORTH & TOWNE**, a ballyhooed chain of stores for boomer women. They nobly tried to respond to the Half Truth frustration of

women 40 and older, who couldn't find any age-appropriate clothes. Women said they were tired of squeezing into midriff-exposing clothes better suited to the 18-year-olds giggling in the next dressing room.

So Forth & Towne designed what they called "grown-up style" stores, that featured "age appropriate" sizing and styling (even age-appropriate associates!), and dressing rooms with flattering, adjustable lighting. But Gap forgot to ask boomers the most important question that would have led to the Whole Truth: "What age do you consider yourself?" Lots of 50-year-olds would answer, "35," which translates to clothes and stores that balance cool *and* comfort. RIP dowdy Forth & Towne.

You may be wondering if I am telling you that women have been lying to you. Not exactly. What really holds you back is everything women aren't telling you—the Whole Truth. Instead, you're buying her Half Truths.

what's a "Half Truth"?

We want to be clear upfront that most women are not intentionally dishonest. A Half Truth is not a lie. A Half Truth is true, but it's not a woman's whole story. This Half Truth telling is generally subconscious, instinctual, or learned behavior. But the subterfuge is so ingrained that it can be tricky to detect when and why she's telling Half Truths.

Just ask a woman, "How are you?" Assuming she's a stranger, she's likely to answer with a reflexive, "Oh, I'm fine." And when probed, she recites, "I've got great kids, a good guy, a nice home. I've got my health. Things are okay." Really? Do you honestly believe that?

She's not lying; she's just given you her good enough answer, her Half Truth. She might be fine, but in her debt-ridden, stressed-out world, she's probably not. A woman who tells you "I'm fine" would rather leave it at that, than admit that she's unhappy, unhealthy, or unfulfilled.

Like it or not, Half Truths are a habit. They're survival gear. They cut the conflict and smooth the way. They're an easy way out. "Yes, I like that dress." "No, it doesn't bother me when you snore." "Yes, I'd love to go to your mom's for dinner (*Again!?*)."

If you think, as a marketer, that you're above being conned by Half Truths, consider how often you've nodded approvingly when female consumers say, "I try to be healthy." How many times have you bought into survey results describing how often women exercise, how carefully they watch their weight, how they've quit smoking, how they always use sunscreen, blah, blah, blah? If the majority of women are so darn healthy, then why is it that the average American woman wears nearly a size 14 (girded in spandex), one in five smokes, tanning beds are still hot, and 82% are so uncomfortable with their bodies that they turn the lights out before sex? "I try to be healthy" is a Half Truth.

Here's the Whole Truth: women exercise (when they feel like it), they watch what they eat (sometimes), they don't smoke (too much), and they wear sunscreen (when they remember).

Half Truths lead to "me too" (or is it "she too"?) products and ideas. So if you create advertising based on this Half Truth, prepare

to waste money on a been-there, ho-hum spot featuring yet another yoga-obsessed woman inhaling calcium pills, when in real life she's consoling her hips with six-packs of high-fat granola bars.

why do women tell Half Truths?

Why do women tell Half Truths? Because they can and because marketers let them.

Despite their desperate need to know what women really want, marketers can actually discourage women from opening up. Most market research and customer feedback techniques run counter to the way women communicate.

Have you ever watched or been part of a group of women when they're with friends? They laugh, tease, touch, share, and generally let it all hang out. Women are amazing communicators, wired to be the more verbal sex. Studies from the book *The Female Mind* have shown that in a typical day, a woman speaks on average 20,000 words while a man speaks on average 7,000. While some scientists argue over the accuracy of the count, it's hard to challenge the everyday evidence. (Plus, it brings to mind the cliché of women's compulsion to ask for directions.) Women ask. Women tell. And women want to be heard.

The question to ask yourself is, "Am I really listening . . . or just Half Listening?"

Contrast the easy exchange of women talking together to the stilted processes most marketers rely on to learn about their female consumers: rigid questions, the formal moderator, the hidden spycam, the dispassionate recording of responses. These techniques fight women's natural impulses to express themselves. On top of that is the penchant for busy marketers to Half Listen. We'll break down these Half Listening dynamics early on in this book so that marketers can understand just how difficult they're making it for women to speak truthfully.

Women have an instinctive ability to know the answer you're looking for. They've spent their lives tuning in to what other people think and picking up visual nuances, body language, and voice cues, whether it's from a demanding teacher, a needy child, or an approaching traffic cop. Like the trained members of a TV studio audience who laugh on cue, women can tell what answer you want from them. And they know how to give it to you, without you even realizing they're handing you a line. And since they sound sincere and reasonable, you believe them and bake those "insights" into brand strategies that can fail.

We want to repeat, women aren't intentionally deceiving you; their Half Truths are simply shortcuts or shorthand so they can get on with their busy lives. A true but halfway response can be a no-fault way for her to evade a tough question or her best effort to deal with the rhetorical, mundane surveys that don't deserve better. Women will save the Whole Truth for those who respect who she is and what her life is about, who ask smarter questions, and who are honestly intent on hearing her answers.

By the way, you may be wondering, do men tell Half Truths, too? While all our research has been focused on women, our intuitive response is yes, but men don't do it as often and their motivations are

not as layered or complex. Women's relationship-driven natures propel their Half Truth telling, whether it's to please, cajole, repel questioners, or protect herself or her family from emotional intruders, like marketers. And women learn to perfect techniques that can keep you from breaking and entering their "consumer space."

the five Half Truths that can shortchange your success

Half Truths are easy for a woman to say and difficult for you to detect. And there's more than one kind of Half Truth waiting to shortchange your business.

After ten years of espionage with female consumers, we've detected five universal emotional drivers of Half Truths—across categories and industries—that can compromise your ability to succeed. These five very female factors help explain how and why women withhold the Whole Truth. Women and marketers play both cat and mouse as they dodge each other and go down blind alleys in pursuit of mutual success. The process of truth seeking and truth keeping becomes a high-stakes game with its own road rules, detours, and potholes. That's why we came up with the acronym GAMES to help keep you on course.

G = Good Intentions
A = Approval Seeking
M = Martyrdom
E = Ego Protection
S = Secret Keeping

1 **Good Intentions** Good Intentions fuel the tendency of women to make promises and profess big aspirations, even with no plan or commitment to achieve them. Simply stating their vows makes women feel more in control of their out-of-control lives. Some Good Intention stories have been told so many times that women start to believe they are true. Marketers fall for this Half Truth because it often matches what they hope to hear, which results in overengineered products and inflated claims.

2 Approval Seeking Women Seek Approval and know how to get it. They'll give pleasing answers to be liked, not only by marketers but also by other women in order to belong and to be accepted. Marketers bite because the answers feel familiar and validate what they think they know about women. When many women chime in, all saying good things about your product or ad (and all hoping to fit in), you're tempted to believe their unanimous opinions and feel discouraged from digging deeper for insights.

3 **Martyrdom** Women, often the productive and responsible caretakers of everybody and everything, deserve to complain sometimes. But they also need you to know that they are doing all the hard work, so they express every detail of their daily hardships and inadvertently try to out-martyr each other. Marketers, also stressed, may find themselves in a "stress competition" with women and miss their need to be heard. The result of this standoff is that women can scare you away from asking them to do anything more, such as buy your product.

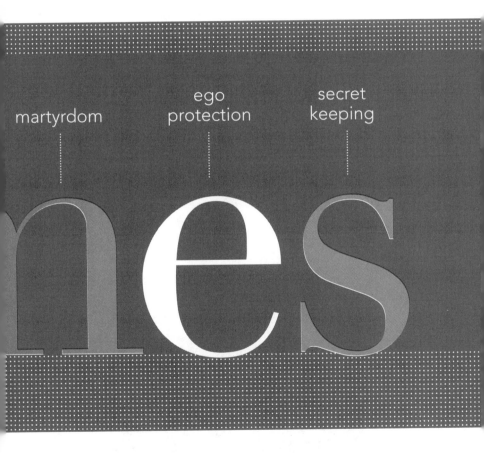

martyrdom   ego protection   secret keeping

4 Ego Protection Women will protect their own inadequacies with pretensions of confidence. They'll pretend to read your fine print. They'll describe themselves as younger, smarter, and trendier than they actually are. And you may believe them because it's more satisfying to market and sell to confident, knowledgeable customers than insecure, uninformed ones. This Half Truth spawns products and services that may overshoot most women's aspirations or be too complicated and then be returned or ignored.

5 Secret Keeping Women use cover stories to defend against interlopers, like you, who may want to collect personal information that will seem shameful when spoken aloud. Thanks to her pride and her protective feelings for those close to her, she'll hide information that invites your disapproval, like her penchant for sneaking cigarettes or even her kids' bad behavior. You won't discover her Whole Truth because you may feel too embarrassed

to ask. And she'll hide some secrets from you that she whispers happily to others as a form of social currency.

Making Half Truth detection even trickier, a simple response can straddle several of the five Half Truths, depending on the question, the setting, and the woman. For example, let's return to the "I try to be healthy" Half Truth. It's a classic Approval Seeking response. But women can also fall back on this Half Truth for totally different reasons.

If you're a healthcare or fitness marketer, "I try to be healthy" is grounded in Good Intentions ("I'm planning to start exercising any day now . . ."). If she's surrounded by a group of fitness buffs but is overweight, a woman might hide behind the Secret Keeping Half Truth ("I've been on Weight Watchers!") rather than admit her yo-yo dieting and exercise habits. And if she senses you're selling appearance-related products, "I try to be healthy" is an example of her Ego Protection kicking in ("If I don't say I'm trying, you'll think I've given up").

Missing or ignoring any of these Half Truths can send you down the wrong strategy or execution paths. In later chapters, we will dismantle the emotional drivers behind these Half Truths, one by one, so you can keep them from sabotaging your new product or ad campaign, as well as your customer service, product development, or retail plans.

how can I get to the Whole Truth?

With all these decoy answers, how can you know what she *really means* and whether she's telling you the *Whole Truth*?

The question to ask yourself is, "Am I really listening . . . or just Half Listening?"

It seems as though it would be easy to listen. But dedicated, single-minded listening is hard to do and hardly anyone does it well. How many times have you simultaneously chatted on a conference call while checking emails, eating a sandwich, and rolling your eyes at your colleague across the desk? That proud multitasking degenerates into chronic nonlistening. (And you wonder why women don't open up to you!)

Deep, engaged listening takes time, which is always in short supply, as well as heart, hard work, and a lot of nerve. That's why we do what we do, so our clients don't have to. Face it, even you, the most conscientious marketer, are reluctant to doggedly pursue the elusive Whole Truth because you'll have to ask women questions that you're afraid to ask. You'll also have to pay attention to her every word, gesture, and reaction like your job depends on it, because it does or it will.

You have to earn your way to her Whole Truth. That starts with listening differently, with all of your senses, as well as your persistence, curiosity, intuition, and, yes, patience, because a woman saves her Whole Truth for the person she trusts. Sometimes, the Whole Truth may be so deeply held that she may not even confess it to herself and may need help untangling what she feels.

This book will open your eyes to a new way of Power Listening to women. We'll help decode what she's hiding and what it means for your strategies so that you can build your brand on Whole Truths for more success and distinction. Once you learn to listen differently, you'll begin to hear what she's not telling you.

why we can tell the Whole Truth and nothing but

If women are so hard to decipher, why should you believe that they've told *us* the truth? For the past decade, Jen, Tracy, and I have refined emotional forensics that defy the "safety net" of the one-way mirror. We've gone one-on-one with women, from Gen Y to seniors, from the shy to the outspoken, from the flip and outrageously funny to the deeply sad and scared.

We engage in emotional forensics.

As partners in Just Ask a Woman, we have listened, eavesdropped, and obsessed over what women think, feel, and buy. Thousands and thousands of female consumers have confidentially confessed their personal stories so that we could help some of the world's biggest brands market and sell better to women.

Leading marketers, manufacturers, retailers, service providers, and media outlets, including **KRAFT**, **GLAXOSMITHKLINE**, **WESTIN**, **BLOOMINGDALES**, **IKEA**, **KAO**, **LIFETIME TELEVISION**, and dozens of others, have commissioned us to be their eyes and ears in the women's marketplace. What we've uncovered has helped these companies make a ton of money and deepen their relevance with their most valuable customers.

We discovered these Half Truths after tens of thousands of hours of interviews and after researching nearly every major product category and most industries (many, multiple times). We began to notice patterns of thinking that were powerful and universal among women, no matter the subject or their income, education, geography, or lifestage. While all women are unique, they also share traits in the way they communicate, make decisions, and react.

For whatever reason, marketers often like to focus more on women's differences, preferring fine-toothed segmentation and consumer algorithms that split hairs instead of commonalities that can actually be marketed to. We think they're missing the forest for the trees. Indeed, there *are* many commonalities, even if these similarities vary slightly from woman to woman or brand to brand, that can help you listen differently, sort through marketing decisions, and better understand why women say what they do and what they really mean when they say it.

These insights emerged from years of qualitative work. In earlier research, we identified female characteristics like otherness (women's affinity for taking care of everyone else first), deliberate decision making (a sometimes slow, but always thorough way of coming to the right answer or purchase), and the predilection for turning to a circle of trusted advisors, a "board of directors," for confirmation of plans and beliefs.

In this research, we looked to build on that knowledge, seeking patterns in the way women communicate their feelings and desires. The result is this analysis of five underlying, universal emotional drivers that can help you decode what women really mean and what they really want.

You might also wonder if these Half Truths differ by age or lifestage. We believe that as women mature, they get craftier about hiding from marketers. Where a young woman may withhold information, it's more about her uncertainty than gamesmanship. Moms in their 30s and 40s are so seasoned from dealing with kids that they can conceal on cue. And boomers have been telling some of their Half Truths so long that they will be expert at convincing you, too.

While mining for women's truths, we've also heard some real whoppers and disclosing them could seem like talking out of school about women. But we're coming clean so that you can be more successful. (And, coincidentally, sharing their Whole Truths will help women get what they really want.)

We offer this note to marketers, particularly women, who may be offended that women are even categorized as Half Truth tellers: Don't take this as an affront to your own honesty. And anyway, this isn't about you, though you might find yourself doing a little silent self-analysis as you read. Rather than vet this book as a Rorschach test of your own truth telling, let yourself take this in and see if this new approach to marketing with women helps simplify and illuminate some blockages with your consumers. And, if you get some insights on your personal life, male or female, then it will be a bonus!

At Just Ask a Woman, we had an ingoing advantage: we're marketers and communicators ourselves and, yes, we're all women. But gender's not enough, since plenty of high-flying female executives will admit that their female consumers can lead them astray (or maybe they don't even realize how their own lifestyles and beliefs may be coloring what they hear from their customers).

What makes us different is the *way* we listen. As you'll learn, we question pretty much every rule of research. We immerse ourselves in women's real worlds every day by devouring their media, reading over their shoulders, snooping in their closets, and road testing the way they shop.

We believe in marketing *with* women, not *to* them as if they were a target to be tapped when you need some cash. By putting women

We believe in marketing *with* women, not *to* them as if they were a target to be tapped when you need some cash.

on our clients' side and engaging them in new ways, we are able to break through to startling, surprising Whole Truths that lead to successful new ways to market with them. Throughout the book we'll share some of these eye-opening techniques for getting women to open up so that you can detect and avoid the Half Truths before it's too late.

Soon, you'll stop asking, "What do women want?" You'll start asking, "What does she really mean by that? Am I accepting a Half Truth . . . or is there a bigger Whole Truth to be found and a bigger innovation or market opportunity waiting for me?"

Next, we'll dig into a case of two well-known marketers: one who bought a Half Truth and stumbled, one who doggedly pursued the Whole Truth and won.

a case of pretty lies

How are Half Truths born and believed? How can women hide the Whole Truth even from the smartest marketers? This is a story about two leading beauty brands, one that pursued the Whole Truth and reaped the rewards and one that was lured into a Half Truth that snowballed into a dead end. Let's begin on a high.

A few years ago, the **DOVE** team at **UNILEVER**, in an effort to expand the brand from bar soap to skin care, turned the beauty business on its ear by launching the "Campaign for Real Beauty," a salute to the natural and unique beauty of women.

Dove decided to break every one of the "road rules" of the cosmetics business. In an about-face from the industry formula of perfect faces, pouty looks, and legs up to there, Dove changed the game. They photographed a half dozen unretouched, clean-scrubbed, slightly overweight women happily wearing nothing but their plain white undies, and then they plastered the pictures on bus kiosks and highway billboards. TV commercials, magazine ads, and Web banners blanketed the country.

The surprising appearance of the Dove "un-models" in fashion magazines and high-impact outdoor media immediately drew controversy for putting "fat women in their underwear" on exhibit and then kudos as the first honest cosmetic ad campaign. (Ironically, the models were actually still thinner than the majority of American women, but no one was owning up to *that* Whole Truth.)

Dove invited consumers to vote online for what real beauty looked like and millions did. The brand introduced the Dove Self-Esteem Fund, a feel-good grassroots program to raise awareness of the link between inflated beauty ads and self-esteem and to educate young women to a wider definition of beauty. One of their later efforts, a viral film called *Evolution*, which graphically showed how images of supermodels are airbrushed and altered, drew nearly nine million hits on YouTube.

Women fell in love with Dove. They hailed Dove as the modern brand built on how women really feel about the beauty industry: disillusioned, disengaged, and dissed.

The verdict was in: finally, someone "gets" what women really want!

realbeautypalooza

When the Campaign for Real Beauty kicked off, newspapers, radio shows, TV news features, and the blogosphere were all over it. Women weighed in with buzz that broke the bank.

Talk shows went crazy. Even Oprah (who, let's face it, has done her share of makeovers) had the Dove women on the show. (Note that the brand was reported to have spent more than $49 million in advertising on Oprah's TV, print, and Web properties over a four-year period.)

The PR value of the "real beauty" campaign was unparalleled, with Dove gaining more than 650 million impressions in the summer of 2005, thanks to coverage on 62 national television programs, devoting the equivalent of four hours of broadcast time, including more than 10 minutes on *The Today Show*. An early skeptic, I was invited to go on *The Today Show* to provide a marketing counterpoint, face-to-face with one of the supernice regular gals from the billboards. I was kind of relieved that I was out of town and unable to do it because I couldn't imagine facing off with someone so universally beloved without seeming like a shallow jerk in front of millions of smitten viewers.

At first, Dove brand's sleepy worldwide sales woke up. (After spending kazillions of dollars, we would hope so!) Even the usually jaded and hardheaded creative ad community genuflected to this heartwarming campaign. They honored "Evolution" with two Grand Prix awards at the Cannes festival of the world's best advertising. Dove received two Grand Good awards at the annual Advertising Women of New York's Good, Bad, and Ugly Awards. And, in tribute to their marketing effectiveness, the campaign won the Grand Effie, the highest industry award for ads that work.

Dove fever was contagious as CMOs everywhere caught Dove envy. (Do you know how many brand managers have said to us, "We want to be the Dove of sneakers/sodas/finance?") You can still go to any conference on women's marketing and hear speakers gush about how they love the way Dove loves women.

The cosmetic kumbaya was complete, except for one little problem: Looking like yourself every day is no reason to buy beauty products. Dove bought into the Half Truth that women want to feel good about their natural looks. It's true, they do. But the Whole Truth is that they really want to look better than they do and that's why they spend $7 billion a year trying.

caught in a Half Truth trap

As women publicly cheered, Dove's second year sales started to slow and then eventually flatlined as the months went on. According to *Advertising Age*, Dove's well-funded 2005 growth of 12.5% fell to 10.1% in '06 and to 1.2% in '07, and the trickle of new products in '08 are a giveaway to the limitations of this platform (not to mention, new rounds of ads that were traditional cookie-cutter, product-as-hero spots).

60%

WE ASK **IMPERTINENT** QUESTIONS

At Just Ask a Woman, we don't mind asking impertinent questions (so our clients don't have to!) because they crack open Half Truths. A beauty-related question we've asked is, "If you were going to your high school reunion, would you rather be told you look gorgeous or look happy?" Although about 60% of women in our poll answered "happy," 40% is a lot of women admitting that they'd rather get a "Wow!" And I'll bet the "happy" ones would be even happier if an unrequited teenage love made a pass.

40%

Half Truth:
"I am happy with my looks."

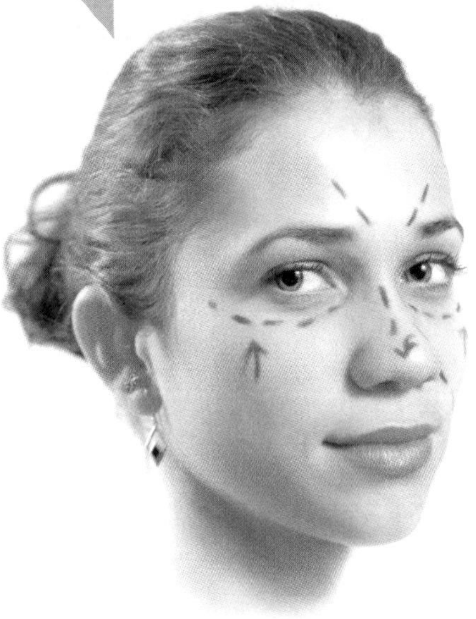

Whole Truth:
"If given the choice, I would like to look better than I do."

While the "real beauty" positioning made strategic sense for basic Dove soap-and-water products, the big money and margin in the skin care category goes to innovations with fancy ingredients and packaging. So, by defining the brand as "you're great the way you are," Dove was hard-pressed to convince women they needed multiple SKUs and the latest science.

How did Dove get in this jam? Because they didn't ask the ugly follow-up questions that would have revealed the Whole Truths, such as "If you like the way you already look, then why do you bother buying beauty products?" Or, "Yes, you feel good about who you are inside, but if you had the choice to look a little better or to look exactly the same, which would you choose?" Sure, those probes would have been a buzzkill in the backroom but they would have saved Dove a bundle.

While Dove's early payoff was a ton of goodwill and fresh awareness for an old-fashioned brand, a huge victory in itself, this Half Truth would make for a short and costly honeymoon. And from a business perspective, it would eventually amount to a very expensive public service campaign about positive self-image.

credit and blame to go around

We were only observers of the Dove story, but I have to believe that plenty share the credit and the blame.

The Dove brand team, confined for years to a simple "¼ moisturizing cream" claim on a cake of soap, must have been excited to see women react so viscerally to the Real Beauty concept. From a strategic perspective, the Dove team was justified in aligning with "Everywoman" based on the brand's heritage as a low-priced soap that's so gentle, it's almost neighborly. At last, the Dove brand, trusted but rusty, had a big idea to hang its hat on.

The marketing team deserves huge credit for boldly supporting the real women idea and moving what must have been a mountain of big-company resistance to change the game. Most companies side with safe rather than risk a renegade strategy.

Likewise, Ogilvy, Dove's ad agency, must have leapt at the chance to shoot a groundbreaking campaign without the stereotypical scaffolding of beauty advertising. Creative directors who make their living pushing cosmetics know the three casting ground rules they're stuck with: skinny, gorgeous, and young. Men and women in those jobs get bored with the same young, same young.

In this rush to real, the team was tempted into believing a lovable (but limiting) series of Ego Protection Half Truths.

- "She looks friendly and normal, not like a scary, perfect model."
- "I'm sick of those airbrushed 18-year-old faces selling me wrinkle cream."
- "I like her because she's regular, just like me."

But there's a difference between making nice and making money. Dove didn't bank on three financial realities.

1. Women want beauty products that make a difference, whether they spend $5 or $500. Dove marketers should have pushed harder for improved results, as well as self-esteem.

2. Skin care and hair care profits hinge on the ability to sell more premium-priced products. Was this "everyday" platform up to that reality?

3. When the heavy spending faded, women could see through the ruse. ("If you tell me I look great the way I am, then why are you still selling me more stuff?")

"She looks friendly and normal, not like a scary, perfect model."

"I'm sick of those airbrushed 18-year-old faces selling me wrinkle cream."

"I like her because she's regular, just like me."

(AT THE RISK OF SOUNDING POLITICAL, SOME WOMEN'S RESPONSES TO VICE PRESIDENTIAL CANDIDATE SARAH PALIN DURING THE 2008 REPUBLICAN NATIONAL CONVENTION WAS VERY AKIN TO THIS: "I LIKE HER BECAUSE SHE'S A REAL HOCKEY MOM, JUST LIKE ME.")

Women love to believe that they look younger than they do. In research we did on haircolor and aging, Tracy asked women to confess what age people took them for. One woman, who was clearly 50 years old or older, said without a shred of guile, "Well, I can pass for 35, maybe 33." If she says so.

And what was the lesson learned? Ask the hard questions, even when you're enamored of "The Truth." Instead, Dove did it again in 2008. Doubling down against that Half Truth would come back to bite them.

fifty-something flop

Year two, the brand stumbled when they transported the real beauty Half Truth into dangerous boomer territory with the introduction of **PRO-AGE**, a line of higher-tech skin care products featuring nude, wrinkled, 50-plus women thrilled to look older. (Get it? *Pro*-Age instead of *Anti*-Age? As in "Hooray, gravity's working!")

We've got to believe that Unilever spent a bundle doing research for Pro-Age. But after listening to women wax poetic about their newfound midlife wisdom, did Dove or their agency probe, "Since you are feeling so great about midlife, do you wake up each day and say, 'Wow, I am so glad I look my age today?'"

There's probably no more annoying "compliment" that mature women hear than this hateful line: You look good *for your age*. And Dove was now saying it right to their faces. Dove confused women's pride in their accomplishments ("I've earned every one of these wrinkles") with their acceptance of their looks as they age.

Showing 30-something women's unclad, imperfect bodies is one thing. Letting it all hang out on a 60-year-old woman in a beauty ad is another. (Hey, we know this isn't politically correct and the idea might work in yogurt or insurance or even home furnishings; but like it or not, this is a category of hope.)

The underlying Whole Truth is that women older than 40 see themselves as much younger than their age. So, the candid imagery of models content to look every ounce and line of their years wasn't what consumers wanted to see in their own mirrors.

Dove gave them no reason to hope for better than what they already had. As cosmetic industry consultant Suzanne Grayson said in an interview with *Advertising Age*, "What they're (Unilever) saying is **The Whole Truth hurts.** that (Pro-Age) is for people who are giving up." So, boomer dollars went to beauty brands that delivered improvement, along with respect.

Lesson learned (again!): The Half Truth of real beauty flies in the face of the Whole Truth of women's hidden vanity and thwarts Dove's long-term brand growth. Although today's women are more confident and self-accepting, they haven't stopped aspiring to be more, especially if they're paying for it.

The Whole Truth hurts.

marketing to her Whole Truth

Like Unilever's Dove, **PROCTER & GAMBLE'S** (P&G) **OIL OF OLAY** was once a low-end, one-horse product, a watery, pink lotion that great aunt Jenny used to keep her skin soft. In the late 80s, Olay broke

Half Truth:
"I'd never go back to being 35. I feel so much wiser now."

Whole Truth:
"Just because I've earned these lines doesn't mean I want to wear them."

emotional category ground with its famous tagline, "I don't want to grow old gracefully, I want to fight it every inch of the way," an interesting counterpoint to Pro-Age's implied "I am old, hear me roar."

Olay realized that it was important to cast models who looked attractive without being intimidating and to speak in language that didn't overpromise. But, as they picked up steam in the 90s, they didn't pitch status quo efficacy. Instead, they marketed Olay to the Whole Truth that women want beauty products that really work.

The Olay product line, with millions invested in product research and packaging innovation, skipped past Dove's Half Truth of Ego Protection and barreled all the way to the Whole Truth. Olay launched Regenerist, marketed as an alternative to invasive cosmetic surgery and billed as the biggest skin care launch in the mass market.

Today, Olay's Regenerist brand and its sisters, Olay Total Effects, Definity, and Complete, own the beauty aisle in pretty much every drug store, with more SKUs than you can shake a stick at. The Olay powerhouses trounced Pro-Age by acknowledging the Whole Truth that women want the results available through professional intervention, but they don't want to spend the money on it or, even more importantly, be judged as artificial.

In 2009, P&G launched Olay Professional Pro-X at department store–level pricing ($69 for a three-product starter set) with the performance promises to back them up. Focusing on the Whole Truth, Olay built an authority platform with sustainable growth and room for innovations that command big bucks. This "results you can see" Whole Truth has propelled the Olay brand to global leadership and dizzying profits, yet they're still perceived as a brand that's on women's side.

Listening to what women say is important. But falling too easily for pretty lies is a mistake. And it all comes down to the way you listen in the first place.

CHAPTER TWO

are you half listening?

H alf Listening, the tendency of busy marketers and retailers to give women their "half attention" and to hear what they want to hear, is rampant and lethal. Whether you're conducting the interviews or analyzing the feedback, if you Half Listen to women, you're building your brand on a shaky foundation.

Every day women are telling you what they love by laying down their hard-earned money and staying loyal to your brand. They tell you what they hate by withholding their wallets, but also by ranting to your 800 lines, blogging about what they don't like, and dressing down a nasty salesperson. And every year, hundreds of thousands of female consumers troop into focus group facilities to be paid for two hours of their in-person feedback. But if you're Half Listening, prepare to get the Half Truths you deserve.

Listening is a tough and demanding job and even the best marketers, under job and deadline pressures, can lapse into settling for convenient Half Truths.

You may have experienced this yourself. You skip out on the research session early, promising to watch the video later, but never do. You're so keen on the idea you are testing that you ignore the women's protests and defend until you win. You gather customer feedback forms but file them under "Later."

Whether we chalk up this Half Listening epidemic to Marketing ADD, a reliance on the same tired questions, or blind adherence to cliché consumer insights, the danger is that you won't hear the Whole Truths you need to succeed.

Most marketers spend as if they have the best intentions as far as listening to consumers—more than $6.7 billion is spent on market research annually in the United States alone. Add to that the cost of hours devoted to reviewing surveys, checking customer satisfaction scores, or training associates in customer care, as well as the millions of air miles and overnights on the road just to "listen," and the dollars

A 50/50 CHANCE

Do you know that many women don't think you are listening at all? One of the saddest questions I ever heard came from a woman at the end of a particularly stimulating videotaped discussion. As I shook her hand goodbye, she looked at me and said, "Do you think that the people who sell this product will even look at this tape of what we said?" I promised her they would, but I have to admit, I'd lay odds at 50/50.

are astronomical. Given that investment, isn't it time to reexamine the fundamental listening practices that are shortchanging success with women?

why focus groups fuel half listening

We lay the blame for Half Listening on the dirty little secret of focus groups, a covert technique of spying on women who are paid to pour their hearts out.

Focus groups rate an F in listening. At Just Ask a Woman, we've dubbed focus groups the F word of marketing, for the literal questions, the stilted dialogue, the monopolizing "talker" in every group, and worst of all, the hostile nonlistening environment in the backroom. Focus groups are like imprisoning women in your own worst meeting.

When a woman who is stuck in one of these stale sessions starts worrying about her endless to-do list and the cost of a babysitter, why would she pour her heart out? It's as if the deck is stacked against getting the Whole Truth. Here's a menu of what's wrong.

The Teflon Moderator

In an effort to engender candor, many moderators will introduce themselves by saying, "I have nothing to do with what I am about to share with you, so you can tell me anything." Imagine whether you'd open up to someone who admits she's the disengaged hired help. It's kind of like going to dinner at someone's house and being told, "Hey, I didn't cook it, I'm just serving it, so if it's lousy, no dirt on me!"

In traditional research, moderators are coached to stay at arm's length from their subjects rather than risk "leading the witness." But in the real world, women open up to people they trust, especially other empathetic listeners who are like them—and ideally, who actually like them.

In contrast to the impartial persona honed by most moderators, Tracy, Jen, and I adapt to the distinct differences of each group. With a group of moms, you can bet Jen will mention her twins. If they're boomers, I manage to let my age slip or use an insider reference that telegraphs our joint experience. Tracy makes sure to dress in a way that is relatable. (You might think this is obvious, but in sessions with middle-class moms, some clients arrive wearing Prada shoes and Gucci pants and then wonder why the women give them the once over.) There's no reason to alienate consumers from the get-go.

The Bugged Room

Another staple of focus groups is the one-way mirror concealing the clients. Don't you think it's weird and disconcerting to be observed by unseen strangers? Women do.

But the moderator lets them know anyway. "Before we begin," the moderator confides, "I need to tell you this room is bugged (our word!). There's a microphone and there are people behind that mirror. They can see you, but you can't see them, but just relax and share with me the story of your incontinence."

No wonder women fall back on telling Half Truths in focus groups just to get through and get out. But the roadblock to Whole Truths isn't the hardworking, long-suffering moderator in the front room. The real problem lies in the backroom. Don't believe us? Come on back.

The Half Listening Lounge

Backrooms are designed for Half Listening, from the food and the amenities to the surveillance and the separation from women.

The focus group facility industry caters to bad behavior, literally. The food and environment are getting fancier by the day. While the consumers out front share a meager plate of packaged cookies, the backroom is cooking up an entirely different menu. Perhaps a hot meal awaits from the cool Asian fusion place in town with chilled Riesling to wash it all down. (We've actually seen respondents sniff the air, noting the aroma of a better meal somewhere just out of sight.)

One facility touts "four kitchens, a full-time chef onsite, available for any dietary needs and culinary requests. At (blank) Research, superior cuisine and high-quality research go hand-in-hand. *Bon Appétit!*"

We've heard of facilities with treadmills for clients to pass the time while listening. One has an ice cream bar in the back, another, a corporate masseuse. Our favorite descriptor came from a big-city facility, where "clients can kick their feet up next to their very own cozy fireplace or gaze out at the skyline . . . like a home away from home." In fact, this facility is delighted to crow that "clients can have breakout meetings and conduct business, all while monitoring ongoing focus group activity on plasma monitors." (Obviously, there's no point in watching for body language or facial expressions that belie her words. Just have a simultaneous meeting and "listen.")

The biggest problem with the backroom is that it's designed to keep marketers and women apart. No wonder Half Truths slip right through.

Talking with Women . . . or About Them?

Once the moderator starts the interview, everyone behind the glass starts to assess the lucky eight women out front who have been recruited, approved, and paid for. You'd think they'd be riveted to every word these women speak.

THE 5 WORST BACKROOM COMMENTS ABOUT WOMEN

1. She can't be our customer.
2. She's fat/ugly/old/dressed like a nightmare.
3. She's not smart since she's not even getting our idea.
4. She doesn't look like she has enough money to shop with us.
5. She can't even give a straight answer. Can we ask her to leave?

Jen's gone as far as keeping a jar where offending commentators are required to drop a dollar every time they insult the women—no kidding.

Instead, the backroom battle begins as soon as the women enter the observation room. Rather than listen, marketers start to talk. Some criticize the respondents with annoyed outrage: "She's heavy/ doesn't even wear makeup/doesn't look like *our* customer!" Some blame the market researcher and become defensive: "Why is *she* here? Why would we select *her*?"

The best listeners don't make assumptions. You never know which woman will give you the insight that will make your idea better. That woman who may not be central casting for your brand may just have the answer you need.

But stereotyping women—assuming the pretty ones are smart, making negative judgments about the unattractive ones before they even speak—is a common mistake. And once you've decided she's not worth listening to, you're bound to miss or ignore the next gem that comes out of her mouth.

But more often, marketers admit that they are passing notes, talking to each other, and even yelling at the mirror when the women don't "get" their idea. Jen has heard some complain that women aren't comprehending the concepts, as if it's the women's fault. "Do women have to have a PhD in your chemistry in order to buy a $4 lotion?" she wonders.

backroom Whole Truths

Are we being hard on focus groups? Rather than be naysayers, we asked 150 leading marketers and strategists about their experiences in backrooms and here's what they told us.

The majority of respondents had ten or more years experience in marketing, ranging from brand manager/director and ad agency account managers to account planners and independent consultants and researchers. And most had attended at least 25 or more focus

BACKROOM **BEHAVIOR**

Once when forced to show concepts in a focus group facility, I could hear the clients whooping it up over everything the women were saying. So I took one of the big idea boards and scrawled on the back, SHUT UP! I raised the board above my head in clear view of the one-way mirror. My message was heard loud and clear in the backroom.

groups in their careers, with 19% saying they had attended "more than they could count."

With that kind of time and money investment, you'd think that they'd be paying attention. Why else would you fly to a city, recruit the perfect group of women, and pay tens of thousands of dollars? Well, it seems that there's a lot more than listening going on. First of all, they were eating. Rather than listening, they were talking, emailing, or tweeting. And a surprising number of these dedicated listeners weren't even in the room! Focus group attendees admitted to playing online games, cleaning out their purses/wallets, sharpening their resumes, generally zoning out, and even napping. (See all the details and stats on the next page.)

As part of this survey, we segmented a group of 50 marketers who attended the 2009 M2W conference, a blockbuster gathering of marketers and communicators dedicated to female consumers. We thought that, as advocates for women, this group would listen better, but their scores were no different than the national average. We asked them to not only rate their own listening behavior but also to comment on what they'd seen their colleagues do. Newsflash! They've seen "others" behave even worse, with 80% seeing others leave early, 36% watching colleagues fall asleep, and 41% cringing while others yelled at the women through the glass. Seems that the only thing most folks are listening to is the sound of their own voices.

So, while women out front are supposedly spilling their guts, the backroom is in a communications free-for-all. Any moderator who's ever visited the backroom to ask her clients if there are any more questions and hears the frustrating comment, "You didn't ask X" and responds, between clenched teeth, "Yes, I did . . . we talked for ten minutes about that!" knows we are telling the Whole Truth here.

Another behavior that respondents confessed is actually something they brag about. Almost 60% said that they are rewriting the

THE HALF LISTENING EPIDEMIC

What were marketers doing in the backroom?

They were eating:

84% ate a catered meal
79% ate M&M's
36% drank wine

They were talking:

73% passed notes to colleagues
67% sent emails
33% talked office politics
27% made a call in the backroom
2% tweeted

And a surprising number of these dedicated listeners weren't even in the room:

67% left to take a call
46% left early to head home

Of those who stayed:

40% daydreamed
12% took a nap

ideas being tested while the women are talking. This could be saluted as a case of proactivity or multitasking, but the fact is that writing while listening assumes there's nothing new to be learned by paying attention. True, if women have trashed what you're showing; premature, if she's just telling you a Half Truth reason that you are accepting too quickly.

what are you asking?

In advance of research, it's pretty standard to develop a discussion guide of questions. But why are those questions often self-serving or just phrased in "marketing speak"?

CAN YOU TYPE AND LISTEN?

Tracy once worked with a company whose marketers resisted the idea of being face-to-face with the consumers. "Why don't you want to be in the room with the women?" Tracy asked. "Because we want to be revising the concepts while they talk," they responded. Why would they start writing before they had heard the whole story and how could they truly listen when their fingers are tearing across a computer keyboard?

L I S T E N

For instance, a packaged goods company recently announced a new logo and proudly described their in-depth research. They asked women, "How do you engage with a food company?" I can imagine women scratching their heads and answering, "By eating?"

No wonder women have started to swat back with the same jargon that plagues corporate life, such as "this copy doesn't grab me."

The best consumer research probes for feelings and beliefs and attitudes, not for final verdicts. But pressured marketers try to milk qualitative research beyond its bounds, even if the responses aren't projectable. Asking women whether they would buy something that's been "sold" to them for the past two hours isn't something to bank on. Asking for a show of hands so that you can take a number of "hoorays" back to headquarters isn't valid, even if it sounds good.

Rather than forcing rankings from women in a conversational environment, try to probe for conviction and relevance and passion.

Try these questions as wrap-ups instead: "When you leave tonight, how would you describe what we discussed to your best friend?" "If you looked into the eyes of the people who run this company and could tell them what you really want, what would you say?" Get ready for ideas you can use.

Power Listening and why it matters

Honestly, most businesspeople seem to prefer the anonymity of the backroom and to leave the asking and listening to someone else. Getting close to women who are judging your ideas is uncomfortable (even for many gregarious marketers), as is listening without commenting, wincing, or criticizing.

But we believe that the Whole Truth emerges face-to-face, with no mirror to hide behind. We pretty much forbid our clients to sit in a backroom—in fact, we hold our sessions in nice hotels where there aren't secret hiding places with one-way mirrors.

The 5 Questions That Beg for Half Truths

1. **"Would you buy this if you saw it on the shelf?"** (Beware total fib attack, answer inadmissible in a marketing courtroom.)

2. **"If this commercial ran on TV, would you stop to watch it?"** (Note: she almost *never* stops to watch a commercial.)

3. **"Is this product for someone like you?"** (If she says, "My sister-in-law would like it," kiss it goodbye.)

4. **"Raise your hand if you think this is something important."** (This is the easiest thing for them to do, and the stupidest thing for you to count on.)

5. **"Let's take a head count of how many of you would buy this idea?"** (A copout for the uncertain woman who will absently nod.)

After sitting next to consumers for the first time, one of our clients said she had never worked so hard to listen.

As testament to the truth-generating power of getting up close and personal, we've noticed that women will approach our clients with personal questions before they leave the sessions. They'll even suggest to clients what "we" need to do to figure out a brand problem. That personal interface is so much more powerful for clients than hiding behind the glass.

Get rid of the conference table when you talk to customers. Retailers can invite a handful of their customers into the store after hours to chat over coffee about how to improve things. Offer to shop along with key customers or take a morning walk with them. We've done it and it's a great way to get the truth *and* a workout.

At Just Ask a Woman, we stretch and reinterpret pretty much every rule of consumer research that we can. We get personal—very personal.

Once when I was asking women about whether they'd consider a particularly gruesome surgical procedure, a skeptical woman asked, "Mary Lou, would *you* do this?" First, I tried the psychologist's twist: "This isn't about me; it's about you." But she shut down, and as I tried to move on, I could feel the question linger in the air. On the spot, I decided to share a story of a medical procedure I had elected to go through. "That was my decision at that point in my life," I said. "Now it's your turn to decide." The room exhaled. The truth flowed.

We challenge women who try to fake us out or tell us what they think we want to hear. We are hands-on, eyes open, and totally female-centric. We have fun. We call them by name, as they do us, and we remember every word they say. (There's nothing more shocking to a woman than when someone remembers what she said a half hour ago.)

We ask the un-askable questions and out them when we feel the Half Truth coming on. And we aren't afraid to laugh with them, cry with them, or admit when we screw up.

The point of Power Listening is to open your mind to her way of thinking, not the other way around. But so often, when we start sessions with some simple conversational openers about what's happening in her life, marketers ask, "Why do we have to waste time on this? Let's get right to talking about our brand." That's not listening; that's selling.

We know women are more open in our formats because when they leave, we've been told more than once by the "pros" (the focus group veterans) that "I really earned my money tonight!" Often, they are relieved to have been so honest. And sometimes, they just thank us for really listening.

That's why women tell *us* the Whole Truth.

what's holding you back from hearing the Whole Truth?

Just as women hide the Whole Truth, you can be guilty of behaviors that block your ability to hear what she has to say. Here are a few examples.

You're drinking your own Kool-Aid. You believe your product is super, so when consumers play that back to you, you pile on. But you may be forcing the consumers to agree with you by asking "Do all these improvements make you reconsider X product?" "Now that you've heard about this new technology, would you be willing to pay more?" It's a big effort for a woman to say outright, "I would never buy this" or "It's not worth the money." You're making it easy for her to fudge.

Women are worn out from being overresearched, so their tiniest indication of enthusiasm sounds like yes to you. We always start our sessions by asking women to raise their hands if they've been in research before. Unless we're in a super remote market, nearly every hand is in the air. When women are listless research veterans, you may be too quick to latch on to any positive response, even if it's just the Half Truth. You've got to resuscitate women out of focus group lethargy with fresh methodologies in order to tap their energy for your product.

Your management loves what you're doing now—or hates it. If your management is tied to an existing idea or restless for a new one, you may feel the pressure to accept a Half Truth before taking the time to get to the Whole Truth. Tight budgets may be driving decisions and squashing long-term initiatives. Today, no one wants to hear about "long term"; "now" is really the only acceptable timeframe. But jumping to the wrong answer won't make your boss love you more.

Your ad agency is really pushing their idea hard. We've repeatedly been in research alongside ad agency folks who become distraught when their idea isn't liked. Are they worried that they can only bring a yes back to the office or that they don't have a backup idea? When

IMAGES ARE POWERFUL

Before conducting research for a dangerous, sexually related health condition, Tracy suggested that the ad agency's sample photos of models representing afflicted women would be a turn-off. Despite Tracy's protestations that the pictures might hurt their idea, the agency resisted, saying they absolutely could not find any pictures of women that were appropriate. "It's just swipe," they said. "It's not what we really mean the end product to be." It wasn't until the consumers in the testing session said that the women looked so "slutty" that they seemed to deserve the sexually transmitted disease that the agency finally backed down.

you feel an agency digging in, you may be tempted to cave and take a Half Truth and run. But female consumers won't care that the agency is getting their way. She's all about her.

If you're honest with yourself, your behavior may also be driven by Half Truths, for instance,

Approval Seeking Have you ever pushed women to say how great your brand is, just so you have it on tape for the higher-ups?

Good Intentions Have you ever insisted on a description of your target customer that is much more intelligent, self-assured, and attractive than she really is, just because you wish it to be so?

Ego Protection Have you ever found yourself describing your commodity product in Nike-esque terms, such as "We're not in the mayonnaise business, we're actually lubricating life?" Get real. It's fat in a jar.

start Power Listening

Let's say you are not behaving in any of the horrid ways we just nailed. But are you a *master* listener? What differentiates the Black Belt Whole Listener from the hobbyist is the ability to listen with your entire mind, body, and spirit.

Power Listening starts with shutting up and shutting down the tech and the voices of your colleagues. Power Listening calls on your eyes, your ears, and your ability to pick up the tiniest variations in someone's voice and body language. And more than that, Power Listening starts with the humility to know what you don't know and the willingness to subvert your opinions for a moment and let women speak.

The best marketers admit they're not the smartest ones in the room. They're not. She is. And if you're not careful, you might accept any one of the five Half Truths that drive her answers. We'll break them down in the following chapters, one by one, so they won't break you.

CHAPTER THREE

good intentions

Anyone who's ever stepped on a scale, tried not to light up, or remade the same resolution they broke last New Year's knows what Good Intentions are all about. "I'll get that report finished early." "I'll hit the gym at lunchtime." "I'll lose ten pounds after the holidays." The Half Truth of Good Intentions gives us all reason to hope.

Female consumers are veterans at these vows of self-improvement. Whether their intentions are as small as daily flossing or as big as scheduling mammograms, women are addicted to these mantras of their "wannabe better" selves (even if, like us, they rarely follow through). Women are optimists at heart who continue to believe that if they say what they intend, someday it will be.

Of course, retailers of quick-fix fitness chains and designers of skinny jeans have gotten rich getting women to pay for promises they don't keep. But for the most part, facing the fact that women's well-meaning wishes are sometimes just wishes will keep you from being left at the altar of her Good Intentions.

If you can't detect the difference between a commitment and a pipedream, it's time for a remedial workshop on this Half Truth. This chapter will examine the difference between women's wishful intentions and their real-life behaviors. We'll look at brands that have detoured around women's vaporware vows and succeeded with stealth strategies, reverse psychology, even flat-out fib protection. We'll share stories of marketers who've learned to accept and then circumvent the reality that a woman may pledge more than she will actually do or buy.

You'll learn how to ask yourself if she means what she says or if she says it to feel good or because she wishes it to be so. Is there code buried in her resolutions that can be leveraged to a great idea? Can I market to the Half Truth of her Good Intentions, even when we both know she has no intention of being that good? In other words, if the road to hell is paved with good intentions, how can I keep my marketing plans from following right behind?

once upon a time, i was on a diet . . .

Let's begin with the example of losing weight, the chart topper of every New Year's resolution list.

When it comes to their waistlines, women are pros at making promises. But they're even better at finding reasons not to keep them: "Last night I said to my husband, 'I'm going to start walking every night.' Tonight, will I go walking? Probably not, but . . .'"; and "I have this mentality of working all week and then on Friday I end up eating a lot of food. A couple of weeks later, 'Whoops!'"

It's not that women intentionally cheat or profess they're on a diet they never started; it's just that life gets in the way.

Half Truth:
"I know that dieting is a lifestyle change."

Whole Truth:
"Tiny portions and calorie counting don't add up to the life I want to live."

a simple truth detector

Women talk a good game of sticking to promises, even if they don't actually follow through. They really do hope to organize their lives, stay on top of their finances, and take control of the unbelievably large amount of time they spend online. So how can marketers capitalize on their Good Intentions without getting shortchanged?

In face-to-face research, the first simple step to eliciting a woman's Whole Truths rests with a one-word question: "Really?" When a woman starts to preach about her rigorous beauty regimen ("I never go to bed without carefully removing my makeup") or how she plans to use all the applications of your new tech toy ("I always read the entire instruction manual first"), try following up with "Really?" in your most amazed, shocked voice. Let the word hang in the air for a moment. It's funny how women will laugh and begin to confess how many times they have strayed and what they *really* do.

Girlfriends are great lie detectors.

Want to see a Half Truth exposed in front of your eyes? In work we did for a healthcare marketer on chronic heartburn, women claimed that they avoided spicy foods. But when they arrived at the research venue, we put them to the test with a covert experiment. We offered a choice of bland turkey sandwich or lasagna with garlic bread. Guess which entrée was decimated? (Proof that they were telling a Half Truth of Good Intentions!)

Try inviting women into sessions with their girlfriends. The pairs of women can be terrific lie detectors for each other, even as they hide their own truths.

And if you find that you're still uncertain if she's confessing her Whole Truth, try some ethnographic techniques. When we've gone to a woman's home to film our ethnographic DocuDiary of her life, there's no hiding the truth in her closets. Or even easier, ask your

Truth in Translation

"I took a vacation from working out when my whole family got sick. (Whether she was exercising before or not, this is a reasonable excuse that engenders empathy.) **I went through an eight-week period without exercising** (relatable) **and it took me another four weeks just to get remotivated. Supposedly I'm on a diet but I just had two bites of brownie.** (It was probably three or four, but who's counting?) **I know better—less in, more out.** (This rote response is on a repeating loop.) **But all of a sudden for the first time in two years, I've gained five pounds.** (Five is too small and forgivable to even mention, so she's probably gained more.) **But I'm getting back on track."** (And when might that be?)

consumers to take their own digital photos or simple videos for an inside peek at their Good Intentions.

IKEA commissioned us to research the state of women's bedrooms. After hearing women describe their bedrooms as well-organized sanctuaries of calm, we asked women to send us pictures. When we reviewed the photos, we were surprised to see the messy Whole Truth of piles of clothes and stacks of paper waiting to be put away . . . someday. These unkept Good Intentions are why IKEA and other retailers like **THE CONTAINER STORE** clean up and a magazine like *REAL SIMPLE* is a huge success. Each is a temple of good organizing intentions where women can experience pathways to neatness nirvana, even if they're just browsing a color-coded fantasy.

give her a cover story

Creating a cover story for women wary of being busted for failing at their Good Intentions is a smart strategy. **MCDONALD'S** is a case in point.

Previously, every time their kids begged for McDonald's Happy Meals, moms either succumbed to their own french fry temptation or skipped lunch entirely. (Don't be misled: if calories didn't count, she would be sidled up next to her toddler with her own Value Meal.) McDonald's picked up on her intention to be "good" by launching a line of fresh salads. These salads might as well have had "mom" written all over them. Adding them to the menu was a genius move to make women feel better about their choice at the Golden Arches. Who cares if the salad is covered in full-fat dressing and crispy chicken (notice they don't say "fried")?

The reason salads worked is that they nailed this Whole Truth: "Every time I take my son to McDonald's, I'm embarrassed that I'm eating fast food, too." Mom felt guilty admitting to her kid-enabled bad habit and she needed a justification for going. Now, mom can say to her friends, "The kids and I stopped at McDonald's, but I just had a salad." McDonald's marketed to the Whole Truth that she didn't only need to save calories; she needed to save face.

The cherry on top of this Whole Truth example is that the salad to-go bag isn't the same, incriminating burger sack but rather a veggie-decorated plastic bag that won't out her as a fast-food-eating slug.

Let a woman give you her definition of her Good Intentions. What's she really after? Does she really want to win an Olympic medal or is she just grateful to make a good effort and get the credit for going for the gold?

help her keep her promises

Women are responsible for more than 80% of their families' healthcare-related decisions. Whether it's for her own health or her kids', husband's, or parents', women are the darlings of the pharmaceutical industry. The healthcare industry, however, is more in tune with the needs of the medical community than the needs of patients. Many major healthcare companies spend little time listening to consumers and, therefore, may not pick up on the difference between what a woman promises and the reality of what she actually does.

A great example of this is the human papilloma virus (HPV) test. Several years ago, a medical diagnostic company developed a test to detect HPV strains that could cause cervical cancer. This test was invented to pair with the PAP, the annual test gynecologists have relied on for decades for cell abnormality detection. This new DNA test was superior in that it could identify strains of HPV that could cause cervical cancer. In our research, women were honest enough to admit that even though they didn't even know why they got PAP tests or what HPV was, they were intrigued.

In-market tracking showed that her Good Intentions were being stalled on the examining table when she faced resistance from the doctors, who were reluctant to do the second test (mostly because it meant more time for counseling, putting longer wait time onto

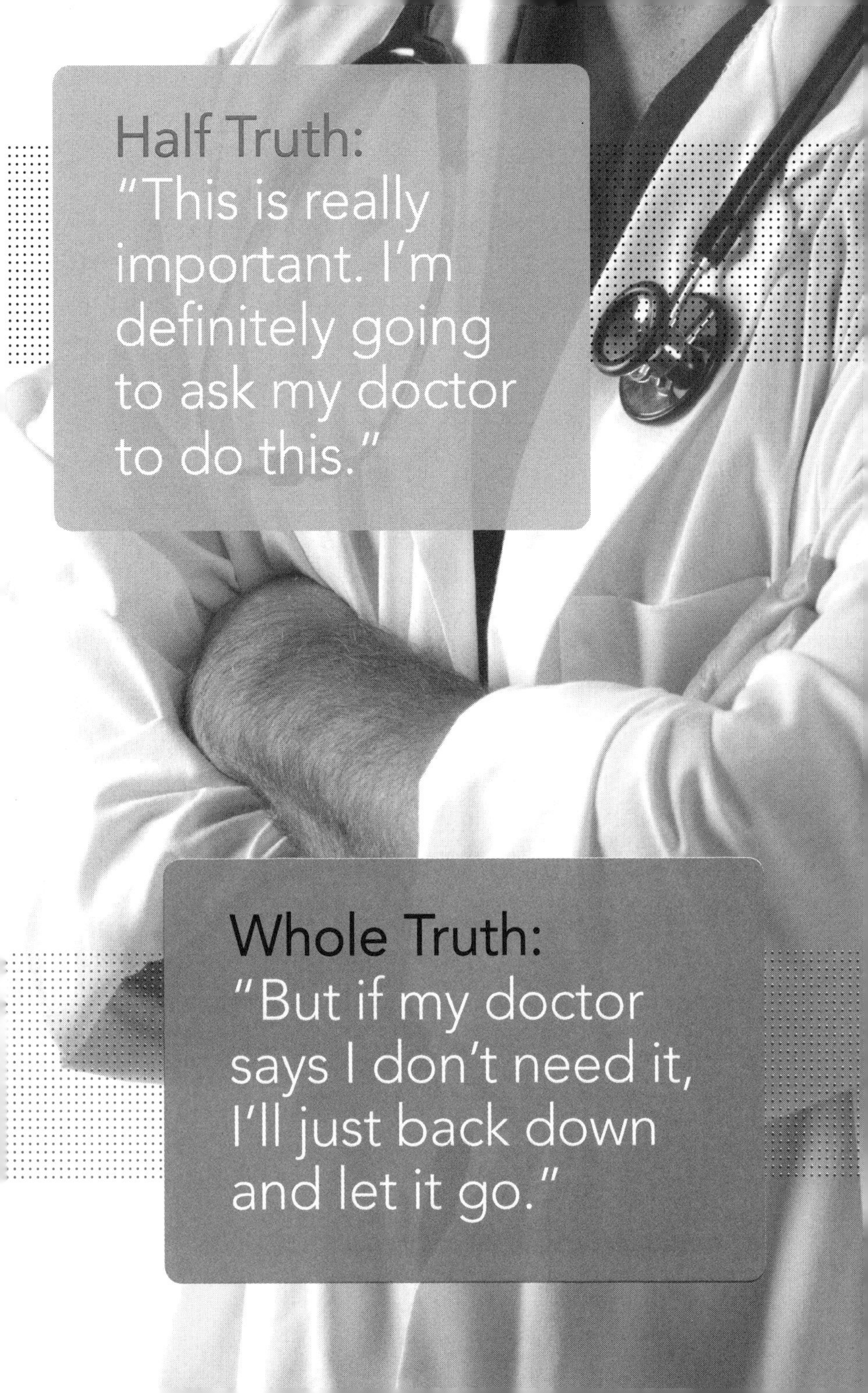

Half Truth:
"This is really important. I'm definitely going to ask my doctor to do this."

Whole Truth:
"But if my doctor says I don't need it, I'll just back down and let it go."

the other patients). So doctors balked and even the most assertive patients backed down rather than argue.

(There's also a bit of Approval Seeking thwarting their Good Intentions, since women hate to raise a conflict with a trusted authority or partner, but more on that in the next chapter.)

So we recommended to our clients that they create a guide for women that would give them the words to say when a doctor said no

In work we did to discover how women researched their healthcare questions, one woman admitted that although she told her doctor that she checked legitimate medical websites, "I really got all my information from an episode of ER."

Think that's funny? In a survey published in the *New York Times*, 35% of women polled said they learned about the HPV Test from an episode of ER, more than twice the number who said they'd heard about it from a doctor. Placing Good Intentions in the right media helps make the most of them!

to their requests for the test—they could keep their Good Intentions and their relationships intact. The company developed an online "script" as an easy way to rehearse the conversation.

The results of this online tool and the concurrent PR were so outstanding that now insurance covers the test, and recent reports claim that the HPV test will soon replace the PAP as the key diagnostic tool for gynecologists. It's not enough to know her Good Intentions; a good marketer helps her keep them.

call it as she sees it

The supermarket shelves are packed with siren call promises of good and good for you. With so many products overpromising whole grains and trans-fat free, it's not surprising that women are skeptical about whether food marketers are partners or saboteurs.

And yet women look for ways to have their chocolate and eat it too. So food marketers plunge in with pseudo-nutrition, like whole grain Chips Ahoy cookies or Splenda with fiber. Both have quasi health/nutrition claims and neither will ever be blessed as good for you. But at least consumers can attribute some small Good Intention as the rationale for indulging a sweet tooth.

To fill this gap between taste and control, **KRAFT** asserted leadership years ago with a new brand based on portion-control packaging, creating a new calorie denomination with 100-calorie packs of products, such as **OREO** cookies. Kraft didn't try to bait and switch women with an envelope containing a single full-size Oreo, knowing the Whole Truth that women customers still needed a sensation of quantity to get satisfaction. So they redesigned Oreos into tiny creamless cookies, to deliver both the beloved taste and extended snacking satisfaction of more than one.

The act of ripping the envelope is enough to restore a woman's sense of control. One weight-conscious woman told Jen: "If I have a

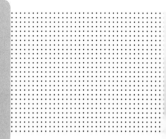

Half Truth:
"I want to eat healthy foods."

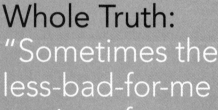

Whole Truth:
"Sometimes the less-bad-for-me version of my favorite foods is good enough."

bag of chips, I'll eat the whole bag. If I eat the whole 100-calorie pack, I get the same psychological closure. I'd never eat two in a row."

Kraft discovered Good Intentions gold: new labeling, new packaging, new psychology. The 100-calorie portions, soon copycatted across categories, simplified decision making and helped women keep their Good Intentions without sacrifice or fear of bingeing. It is perfect Whole Truth marketing.

smoothing the way to her Good Intentions

Women's Good Intentions are often foiled due to the "yucky/boring" factor of doing the right thing. How can you spin some marketing sugar to make the medicine go down?

Let's stay with food for a moment. Women might say they know they need more fiber but they associate it with gritty dull flavor. Products like **FIBER ONE** have penetrated the women's market by pumping the brand's fiber content into pancake mix and Pop-Tart-like treats, a great way to make a tasty treat good inside, too.

In various categories, marketers have found ways to navigate women's Half Truth Good Intentions by making them more fun.

For instance, many moms want to spend more together time with their kids, but are roadblocked by video games. Though a mom might say she wants to play, the Whole Truth is that she often has neither the interest nor the time to learn. Enter **Wii**, with a portfolio of games, sports, and now WiiFit, all geared not only to engage women with their families in fun activities, but also, and even better, to increase the utility of a device that was sitting dormant in homes from 8 a.m. to 3 p.m.

Another Good Intention that women profess but don't act on is learning simple home repair. The growing numbers of single women and the many women whose husbands don't even watch HGTV fantasize that someday they'll install their own bath tile or new lighting. **HOME DEPOT**'s Do It Herself workshops provided the perfect way to put the fun of an all-female DIY training session right in the stores. The classes were a way to help women not just dream, but actually do—and then of course, spend. With the economy encouraging more DIY projects over paying professionals, this strategy is starting to pay off.

taking the long view of short-attention intentions

One of the critical Good Intentions that too many women profess is the plan to get their finances under control. If there's anything the recession of 2009 taught us all is that money that's taken for granted is soon taken for good.

Women unfortunately will talk a good game about money, but the reality is far different. They'll say, "I really think that this year I will put in the time to educate myself about my money management." Too often, the Whole Truth is, "I haven't even made out my will, let alone have a clue where to start." While men are quick to pull the trigger on these decisions, women tend to be more deliberate and examine options and even delay signing on the bottom line until they are certain they are taking the right step for themselves and their families.

So women will start collecting and coding paperwork or checking out advisors, then stash it all for a rainy day. This stop-and-go procrastination has frustrated even the best financial services marketers who don't have the patience to wait for women. Insurance companies like **STATE FARM** and **FARMER'S INSURANCE** decided that the dollar potential of the female audience was worth taking the long view and have created vibrant websites for women that serve as a resource for whatever stage of financial readiness women are in. In addition, hiring female agents and featuring them in TV commercials have helped demonstrate that State Farm wants women's business, whenever they are ready to follow up on their intentions.

AMERICAN EXPRESS created OPEN as a way to support small businesses but quickly recognized the power of women in this market; so year after year, the company has sponsored events for networking and skill building as a feeding ground for new accounts. They've hooked up with Nell Merlino's "Make Mine a $Million Business," a not-for-profit group that helps female entrepreneurs succeed through financing, education, mentoring, and marketing help. Expecting immediate results, as too many financial companies have done and then failed, ignores the slow path to her Good Intentions.

Expecting immediate results ignores Good Intentions.

build a brand out of failed Good Intentions

Women's beauty drawers are the graveyard of failed Good Intentions, from abandoned skin care regimens to tricky eyebrow kits. The proliferation of two-in-one products, fast-acting creams, and long-lasting formulations all testify to marketer's success at supporting her Good Intentions.

Women know they should wear sunscreen every day, but don't. So cosmetic marketers pour SPF into everything from lip balm to hair conditioners, so women can live with their broken promises, even if the SPF "dose" is barely effective. Women claim that they wash their makeup off every night, except if they're out late, too tired, etc., etc., etc. No wonder mineral makeup brands have gained a reputation for being so good for your skin you can sleep in them and actually improve your looks—it's incredible marketing sleight of hand!

Sometimes women need an easy way to keep their bad beauty behavior undercover until they can make good on their intentions. In research we've done on hair color, women claim to color as often as every four to six weeks to keep up with root regrowth, when in reality, many wait three months or longer. If confronted (a mirror will do!), women will blame their delays on the time required and pretend that a baseball cap can conceal their procrastination.

Like many marketers, **CLAIROL** may have been reluctant to give women a way out of buying a new box of their product. But when it was evident that women were dabbing on their full-size product inappropriately, they came up with a solution: the Nice 'N Easy Root Touch-Up kit, a way to help women pretend they color religiously, even though they don't. The product is a blow-away success because it allows a woman's Good Intentions to stay intact.

making her Good Intentions work for you

Maneuvering around the landmines of this Half Truth does not mean giving up on aspiration; it does mean that marketers need to navigate the bumpy waters of ego, excuses, and ever-changing promises to discover the Whole Truth underneath.

As you look at your category or business and try to apply these lessons to your consumers, avoid being undermined by a woman's Good Intentions and turn her promises into your profits.

Give her permission to fail,
ways to keep her promises
painlessly, and the chance
to save face.

how to avoid the Half Truth of Good Intentions

1. Her Good Intentions are not necessarily what you think. Let her express her needs for your product or category in her words, no matter how inflated, then push her to answer the question, "Really?" to be sure she isn't hiding her real desires. Her definition of what being good means in your category is what matters, not yours.

2. Give her permission to fail, ways to keep her promises painlessly, and the chance to save face even if she doesn't comply with all of your "rules." Remember, she's trying to do her best by buying your product and that's what counts. Don't make your subterfuge obvious; she will see that you "get" her just by the shortcuts you offer to her intentions.

3. If you fake your way into her favor and then fail her Good Intentions, prepare to be found out. It's less risky to create something she will count on and tell friends about than to give her a reason to mistrust you the next time around.

CHAPTER FOUR

approval
seeking

Finally the day has arrived when your ad agency is presenting new creative work for your leading brand. While they're a little past deadline, the team is excited and so are you. (Though you might not admit it, you're wearing your cool jeans and boots that give you that "I'm hip enough to be taken for an outside agency creative" look.)

The copywriter and art director begin their pitch, and though they show lots of ideas, you can't find a single thing you like. But you know that this team has hit home runs before and you don't want to deflate their balloon too quickly.

"So, what do you think?" they ask hopefully (though they're already preening like they're advertising rockstars).

"There's a lot of work here, that's for sure," you say (a timeworn dodge that passes for the positive answer they want to hear).

"We all really loved the last two boards best," they say (trying to build a quorum of creative love).

"Yeah, the celebrity bit is funny if we can afford it," you offer (an easy out until you ask their boss for a total do-over).

"Great meeting! We can't wait to start working out the production details" (an agency tactic to build the pressure to agree).

"Hey, did you catch *Entourage* last night?" (a trick to change the subject to keep the friendly vibe going).

If you see yourself or a colleague in this story, you know what this chapter is about. The Half Truth of Approval Seeking is the collection of covert behaviors, such as faked chumminess or clever diversion, designed to build consensus or get along. Whether we dress to impress, stretch to find common ground, minimize differences, or flatter our way to yes, these everyday approval-seeking behaviors aren't that dangerous. But they can be deadly for marketers. When women resort to this Half Truth instead of coming clean with what they really feel and want, they can thwart your marketing success with a smile and you won't even know it.

> Seeking Approval is a natural instinct.

Seeking Approval is a perfectly natural instinct, a way that human beings pursue affiliation. If you are protesting, "I don't care if I'm liked!" (how often do you tell yourself *this* Half Truth?), then you are probably alone more than you care to confess.

In the situation at the start of this chapter, let's assume that you're tempted to yell, "These ads stink. You're fired!" But rather than descend into a downward spiral of spite, you, a seasoned marketer, instead find a way to preserve the relationship and then work the system before throwing in the towel.

It's important that you understand how significant and motivating Approval Seeking is to women. In general, women are keenly driven to belong and they sense how others see them. They will turn themselves inside out in an effort to find something good, even in your bad idea. Likewise, they are attuned to how you regard *them*. In their interactions with your brand (and if you are a retailer, with your store), their antennae are wired for details and nuance, all the small signals that demonstrate either respect or rejection. Just as they are tough judges of themselves, they can be tough on you; yet in their quest to please, they won't always tell you you've crossed a line until it's too late. In this chapter, we'll identify three minefields where women's Approval Seeking can either derail or deliver results for your brand: market research, brand development, and at the moment of truth—at the register, in the showroom, or on the website where she buys your product or services.

why women seek approval

Before we begin, let's explore why women seem especially prone to Approval Seeking. Psychologists have studied the effects of "social anxiety," which occurs when people are concerned about how they're evaluated by others. Social psychologists have noted the incredible power of the need to belong and its companion, the fear of social rejection. We often observe how far women will go to earn an A or to avoid an F from others.

Many researchers believe there are two different aspects of this social self-consciousness: private (the running tape in her head that continually asks "How am I feeling?") and public (the self-awareness meter of how she's perceived externally: "What do they think of me?"). The higher her level of public self-consciousness, the more likely it is that a woman will focus on the opinions of everyone else, while carefully trying to avoid criticism.

In our experience, and perhaps in your everyday life, you may have noticed that women seem to strive for social validation more than men. (Otherwise, why would overweight men strut the beach in Speedos while average-size women cover up in sarongs?)

Even when they are complimented, women will fixate on whether the kudos are genuine, and they will hoard a personal slight far longer than it's worth.

Women will share the story of a bad experience with four to seven others, but they've been known to repeat a really hurtful incident for as long as 23 years. Avoiding criticism becomes a full-time job.

it starts with market research

At the market research stage of a project, women will display their Approval Seeking skills in an effort to avoid sticking out and to improve their odds of securing support. They will try to get along even though they disagree, and likewise, they will all silently agree to hate something even if individually they don't. Now, imagine yourself in the back room as all the women pile on the criticism train and you're trying to keep your agency calm while their work is being gang-ripped through the glass. Your agency colleagues are in their own approval search because everyone likes to feel liked (even if they aren't). Ironically, all this faux agreement has the opposite effect, pitting you against consumers and blocking your ability to listen.

The Frustration of Too Much "Yes"

In research, it's common to see women robotically nodding at each other, acquiescing to whatever the moderator asks of them or whatever the self-designated "group leader" insists is true. They'll even pleasantly pledge to buy what you're selling. But rather than be delighted, many marketers become skeptical, even ticked off by a group of female consumers who agree with each other.

Many attribute a round of unanimous yeses or nos to mob mentality and are quick to claim that women in research are victims of groupthink and to discard what they've said. This is a big mistake.

If you believe they love your idea in research, you risk launching a loser no one really likes unless you got lucky with a good idea. And if you believe nothing they say just because they all agree to love or to hate your idea, that misconception will also come back to bite you.

The allure of too much agreement in research is that you are lulled into believing women mean what they say without challenging it. Even if a chorus hates your ideas in unison, there's always the reality that a few in the room like the ideas. That's why when we listen to women, we break the approval cycle. In our talk-show research

Your brand can get hurt if you fall for the notion that all the women love your idea *or* if you dismiss their opinions as **groupthink**.

format, Just Ask a Woman LIVE™, we keep our eyes trained on the most timid woman in the group while challenging the big talker who's getting all the head nods, catching her when she contradicts herself so that the quiet woman gets up the nerve to speak out.

What you learn from market research will either anchor your brand to a strong, provocative foundation or send it down the slippery slope to an acceptable but boring nowhere. Don't settle for gratuitous smiles. Never, ever let women off the hook, even if it means confronting their enthusiastic yeses or dour nos with a "Do you really believe that?" It's worth ruffling feathers to achieve what's right for women and your brand.

In our work, we face this Half Truth right up front. We always begin our sessions by saying, "While we're together for the next couple hours, let's agree to disagree. You can all sing 'Kumbaya' in the hall when this is over." We always get a knowing laugh, since women are onto their own game.

Screening Yourself from the Truth

Approval Seeking comes with the territory of market research. More than that, you might be surprised to know that you unintentionally bring it on yourself. What else would you expect but agreement from a group of eight moms, aged 35 to 40, all with young kids, some college education, household income between $40,000 and $55,000, living in the same neighborhood, and suffering from migraines? Of course, they get along and think alike! You personally cast them that way!

Your accomplice in creating an "all yes" atmosphere is the screener, the questionnaire that recruits the "perfect" set of women and screens out differences of experience, opinion, and personality. Paid recruiters tally up family status, income, education, media habits, product consumption, even answers to attitudinal questions such as, "Are you someone who thinks of herself as creative?"

SCREENED OUT

Jen was conducting a session on health care in Kansas City and, scarily, a woman in the group had a seizure. Everyone froze. Jen ran out of the room into the hotel to call for help. The EMS folks arrived quickly and attended to the suffering woman. (She was ultimately fine.) During the commotion, the client said, "I can't believe that no one in this group was a nurse or medical worker who could have helped." Jen sighed. "That's because you screened them all out!"

Many women, in turn, give good enough answers, especially if they really need the money paid for making the cut.

How hard is it to be accepted for research? We've seen 17-page questionnaires. If you answered your home phone at night while the kids were trying to get your attention and the dog was out of control and someone asked you 17 pages of questions, what are the chances you'd (A) stay on the phone, (B) answer each question thoughtfully, and (C) tell the Whole Truth to a perfect stranger? The answer is D. You'd hang up.

Still, marketers rely on screeners to be absolutely sure that all the *right* women are in the room (aka all those who share the same problems or carry the same prejudices), so no wonder all the women agree, or disagree together, as much as they do. You cloned them to be identical.

Screeners also eliminate anyone with any knowledge of the subject, especially if they have marketing experience. If anyone has an odd predisposition toward the category, then she's thrown out, too. Though screening is necessary to guard confidentiality and to kabosh women who fundamentally hate your brand, some screeners border on the absurd.

Still, women sometimes slip through by concealing what would keep them out. Even with our scrutiny, we've had outliers, like the woman who wore scrubs to a medical interview, or another who brought her oxygen tank to a session on fitness.

You might think that online surveys would elicit honesty and stifle the reflexive yes factor. But in online screening questionnaires women can guess the "right" answer pretty easily after a couple of questions. In a recent online questionnaire I was using to recruit women to appear onstage with me, the first respondent described herself as witty and outspoken. The second woman had checked the exact same thing. The third, ditto! Could they all truly be witty and outspoken? It was clear that they had just checked off the responses to get chosen for a good gig. With no one to monitor the truth of her clicks, imagine how many Half Truths you might be buying when you use online surveys as a substitute for in-person research!

Get real about the screening process

To get the right women into research in the first place, marketers need to get real about the screening process. Here are some helpful tips to avoid research sabotage: Challenge your team to shorten your screeners so smart people won't hang up on your research invitation. Stop worrying if the women have ever worked in marketing. The ones who have will be quicker to get what you're talking about.

Too many screeners focus nearly every question on insider details rather than on discovering those personal qualities that can prevent the epidemic of too much agreement. Rebalance your screeners to recruit for women who will speak out, be creative problem solvers, and withstand the strong opinions of others. Choose individuality over "Miss Congeniality" so you'll find someone bold enough to disclose personal stuff even if it ticks off other women in the group.

Finally, give yourself a deeper insight into the women in whom you're investing market research dollars and time. We ask women to do homework before the assignment as a way to gauge their creativity and real association with the marketing problem at hand. Time and money well spent on screening upfront will pay handsomely in the truth you need down the line.

deciphering the meanings of "yes"

The Half Truth of Seeking Approval is fraught with confusion. Think of two women playing a game of indecision with a restaurant lunch menu, until one cops out with, "Okay, I'll just order whatever you're having." By being so noncommittal and agreeable, neither gets what she really wants. Here are some ways women condition their yeses rather than 'fess up.

She Agrees, Sort Of

In our research for this book, we asked marketers which focus group responses really drive them crazy. These approval zingers zoomed to the top (with some translation from us):

- **"I agree with her."** (Please like me because I just supported you.)
- **"This is just my opinion, but . . ."** (I am not disagreeing, just stating my insignificant, different idea, which you can ignore.)
- **"This isn't my experience, but others may feel . . ."** (Even though I disagree, I am going to make everyone else feel like their ideas are smart.)

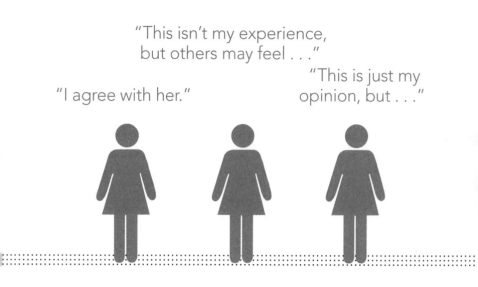

"This isn't my experience, but others may feel . . ."

"I agree with her."

"This is just my opinion, but . . ."

We often remind women to answer for themselves, not the mysterious "other" women they defer to. We cut in with, "I'm not asking about other women, I'm asking what do *you* want?" We call them up short and honesty follows.

She Avoids Saying No

Despite the obvious physical gestures of camaraderie and interest, women's language tells a different story if you listen carefully.

I'm guilty of this myself. When faced with youthful indecision, my mom always coached me: "Just say yes. You can always say no later." This still comes in handy. And it works for a lot of women in market research who know that by seeming to agree, even if they disagree, they can stay in the inner circle that's been created.

Rather than risking criticism for a negative reaction, a woman might employ various strategies to say no without uttering the word. Here's how:

Half Truth:
"Sure, what she said."

Whole Truth:
"It's easier to say yes than to tick off that bully woman or drag this group on any longer."

- **She ducks the question:** "I think this product would be great for camping." (I've never gone camping, and I never will.)
- **She likes your product on someone else's behalf:** "I think this would be great for my sister." (My sister's not here, but she'll buy anything.)
- **She puts a price caveat on her yes:** "I'd really like this as long as the price was low." (She would only buy it if the price were so low that you'd never make a dime.)
- **She sits it out:** "I don't know. I'd have to do more research on this to tell you what I think." (I'd rather not trash your idea on the spot, so I'll pass.)

products based on belonging

Some marketers co-opt the concept of women's desire for affinity and leverage it for product success.

An example of a brand whose success hinges on helping enable women's desire to connect is **WEIGHT WATCHERS**. While the brand understands the Half Truth of acceptance of like-minded peers, they recognize the Whole Truth, that the badge of membership is as important as actually following the regimen. Women claim compliance with the point program (even if they're not), and when they reach their goal weight, they will cling to their record book for years.

The Weight Watchers brand is proof that a support network of women who all share weight challenges yields results. In addition to the meetings, the online community expands access to the club as a place for learning real-world tips, admitting trip-ups, and sharing solutions. The brand also carries a seal of "righteous effectiveness" so that advocates can pass along the endorsement that "only Weight Watchers really works" or is doctor-approved, burnishing their Approval Seeking halo.

Half Truth:

"I want to fit into the group I aspire to."

Whole Truth:

"Even though I want to belong, I don't want to be a clone."

Weight Is Contagious

A study from Harvard medical researchers and the University of California, San Diego showed that gaining or losing weight is "contagious" among overweight friends. The more excuses are shared, the more everyone gains weight. The more support within the circle of friends, the better the loss. Women, as the gender more likely to diet, know how susceptible they are to jumping on the bandwagon of their friend's broken promises.

But the real genius of attaching this clubby feeling to a product is to recognize the bigger Whole Truth that although women crave belonging, they also want to feel unique within the group.

The **MINI COOPER** can trace its success with women to tweaking this clubbiness with a twist of personalization. Driving a MINI Cooper says she belongs to a smart, fun group of energy-conscious, stylish, quirky folks. A woman might join one of their cross-country rallies, but her customization makes the car hers alone and, in essence, allows her personality to shine.

Smart marketers are realizing that women actually like to flaunt their unique differences and even "bad" behavior. **FRITO-LAY'S** Flat Earth, Lay's Chips, and Smartfood teamed up to create "Only in a Woman's World," a site that features four women and their idiosyncrasies, which allows visitors to play games with the virtual women, imagine their snarky comments, even send e-cards reflecting their unique spins on life.

Just because two women are moms doesn't mean they are blood sisters.

bringing sisterhood to brand development

Another big Approval Seeking manhole or opportunity in product development is the trap of sisterhood, where marketers, having observed how connected women are when together, try to tap into the value of that "sisterhood" for their brands. But they may be over-reaching when they assume that just because women are alike, they want to be clones.

While marketers see the power of women online, especially on social-networking and shopping sites, all's not sweetness and light in cyberland. Women are tough judges of just who gets to be in their approved circle. Look at how a wedding website like **THEKNOT.COM** works for women. You might think that all brides have a bond and that all advice is created equal. Not so. When Jen was getting married, she'd check out pictures of the happy couples before she took their decorating ideas. If the brides looked tacky or their taste was questionable, Jen wasn't so eager to sign up for their florists.

Here's how misinterpreting this feel-good Approval Seeking Half Truth steered some brands wrong—and some right. Women can get ticked off when you assume affinity they don't really feel. For instance, hotels set up all-women floors, largely in the name of security. But women business travelers, especially those traveling with male colleagues, don't want to come off as separate or wimpy and certainly don't want to be embarrassed at the front desk with a key that says, "Women floor only."

Interestingly, some women's travel websites have stumbled by going too pink, suggesting book clubs and cute woman-y tips that leave professional women annoyed. Women aren't looking to join the sisterhood of the traveling laptops, they just want to get where they're going.

In 1995, **WYNDHAM HOTELS** was the first hotel chain to launch a women's initiative, "Women on Their Way," and recently updated the program to make it even more right for women today. While they offer an online community and blogs for bonding and commiserating over the trials of travel, most of the program serves women's self-interests, like special deals, destination information, and shortcuts to make travel more bearable.

Another approach to this is the way that **KIMPTON HOTELS** create a women-friendly oasis. In addition to offering female-centric amenities like static guard and eye-makeup remover pads, Kimpton allows guests to leave a small bag of their toiletries at their frequently visited properties. (And since women carry five times the products men do, that's a big benefit!) And for all the women who'd like to relax together at the end of a busy travel day but dread the typical hotel bar scene, Kimpton offers Wine, Women, and Fun, an end of day wine hour for women only.

Approval Seeking at the register

It's one thing for a market researcher who's got two hours to interview a woman to figure out her motivations or for a brand manager to synthesize the insights from thousands of women for months at a time. But at the point of sale, the typical associate or agent or website gets just seconds to assess her yes, so no wonder there are so many snafus. Getting your messaging right at the point of sale calls on your ability to be fast on your feet.

Retailers in technology, financial services, automotive, and even health care wrestle with what women really want and can discover too late that a woman's tacit approval disguises a customer on the verge of meltdown. Salespeople don't understand that a nodding woman isn't the same as a nodding man. A man will generally nod when he means he agrees. A woman will nod to acknowledge that she hears what you're saying, but by no means does it guarantee assent. Only direct follow up such as "Now that you've heard what we're offering, are you interested?" will get you closer to that truth.

When women feel rejected or disrespected, they can use their Approval Seeking skills to get their way. In work we did for a major insurance company, a particularly sweet, unassuming woman described how she'd been ignored by her agent after he'd smooth-talked his way into a contract. She tolerated his unresponsive service for months on end, until she finally called and asked for him under the guise of a friendly follow-up call, only to tell him that she was firing him for incompetence and wanted him to know it.

In research about car buying, one young mom calmly stated her tactics for dealing with the frustrating runaround in the showroom: "When I shop, I usually bring my children along. And I keep an eye on them. But when the salesman starts the 'I've got to talk to my manager' runaround, I don't control my children anymore."

She Sees Through "Fake Sincerity"

Some companies go overboard to satisfy this Half Truth of feeling respected and liked. And faux friendliness falls as flat as the über-cozy waiter oozing, "My name is Jason and I can't wait to serve your table tonight." Uh-huh.

Thinking that prescribed small talk will pass muster with women is a big mistake. Veterans at making nice, women are expert at sensing insincerity. The authentic support women want is exemplified by the customer service reps at **LANDS' END**, who will actually try on a

SCRIPTED EMPATHY

Jen shares this recent experience with the **T-MOBILE** customer service representative after she had a **BLACKBERRY** meltdown: I predicted a long, frustrating call after navigating out of the voice-automated system, but I was quickly greeted by the world's happiest young woman. "It's a great day at T-Mobile in BlackBerry Support, how can I help you?" After I gave my name, rank, and serial number, I told her my problem, which sent her empathy into overdrive. She chirped, "That must be just awful to be inconvenienced like that. I am so sorry that this happened to you, and we will find a way to fix it right now." She was reading from the world's most patronizing and annoying script. I was tempted to ask about the weather to see if she could answer a question without the script. She put me on hold for a millisecond and came back with, "I am *so* sorry that I put you on hold. I know that your time is important and waiting can be frustrating." It took her longer to apologize than I had been on hold!

pair of shoes while you're on the phone to tell you if they run large. Even better, a representative from Lands' End called Jen just to let her know that she was granted free shipping for a month as a reward for being a good customer. That's a way to get her approval for good.

Later, we will focus on how this Half Truth and others run rampant at retail, but it's important to acknowledge that women expect that a brand will get it right end to end. And to a marketer, that means that a powerful research insight that infuses a product with differentiation and value must connect with women in an ad or on a shelf or online. All that came before is moot if she doesn't see her Whole Truth when it's time to buy.

how to avoid the Half Truth of Approval Seeking

1. Stop fighting groupthink. Affinity among women helps them confess what they don't want to tell you. Just be sure to dig deep enough to understand what's really behind her yes or no.

2. Before you let the Approval Seeking truth seep into your product idea, don't force her into "clubs" she doesn't want to join, or at least find ways to acknowledge her uniqueness in the group.

3. At the moment of sale, watch out for the temptation to read her yes as agreement or to overdo the nicey-nice talk. She can spot fake approval, because she's so good at giving it.

CHAPTER FIVE

martyrdom

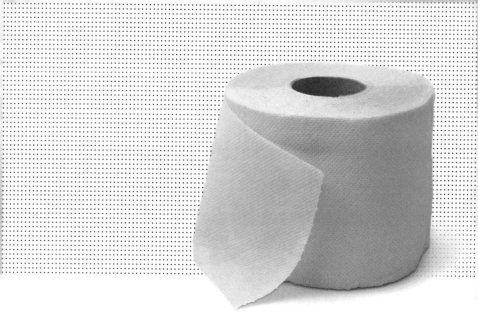

"I just wish I didn't have to repeat myself a million times a day. If I could only record myself and just play the tape over and over . . . Like, 'If you eat that piece of cheese, the wrapper doesn't just stay on the counter, you throw it away.' And why am I the only one who can see that the pile of laundry at the foot of the stairs needs to be taken up? And what about the toilet paper? Sometimes I'm sitting there thinking, *Why can't anyone else put toilet paper on the roll?* Someday I'm gonna make the whole family come and sit down and we're gonna have a lesson."

welcome to her worst day ever (so far)

Ask a woman about her busy life and you'll be smacked in the face with the realities of her never-ending to-do list, the marker of Martyrdom. The Half Truth of Martyrdom is women's irresistible need to express and describe the minute details of her daily stresses so that others understand just how overworked and sometimes overwhelmed she feels.

she has a right to complain

Women *are* the gatekeepers, family doctors, caretakers, shoppers, and wallet watchers of America, even as more men, especially Gen Y dads, start to pitch in. With increasing numbers of single moms, divorcees, and widows, there are more women left holding the bag.

Just as the legendary martyrs endured bizarre, medieval torture as sacrifice for the greater good, women grin and bear it while compensating for everyone else's deficiencies, from the smallest irritation, such as the empty toilet paper holder, to the bigger issues of their family's welfare. But even the most capable women can't conceal the frustration that bubbles beneath the surface, ready to erupt. Yet, underneath the resentment, women are proud and even possessive of their role as chief operating officer of the household. Here's an example of a woman's pride and unwillingness to delegate: "We have our own business and I run it. I wake up between 4:30 and 5:00 a.m. to get everything done. We have four children, three schools. It works better if I'm the one multitasking because I have more patience. But I'm mentally tired."

A woman's motive for voicing Martyrdom to marketers isn't to get rid of responsibilities. She just wants to be heard. In a survey on Parenting.com, 60% of moms feel they don't tell their friends what they're going through in their lives, so they crave someone—anyone—who will listen.

When women wax on about their sacrifices, marketers react in one of two ways: They shut down because they really don't want to deal ("Not my department!"), or they go overboard with sympathy and stumble headfirst into her rage.

An example of this is the public flogging of **MOTRIN**, the analgesic marketed by the **MCNEIL CONSUMER HEALTHCARE** division of **JOHNSON & JOHNSON**.

Motrin had developed a strong profile among moms by positioning itself as "Mom's Motrin," solving the aches and pains that come from the physical strains of raising children. Their brand personality was well matched to women's truth: in control and impatient with pain that interfered with busy motherhood. But a single commercial where they tried to apply that brand empathy to new moms got slammed in the blogosphere and bashed in mainstream media. Motrin seemingly interpreted the Half Truth of Martyrdom too literally with a well-intentioned ad that focused on baby slings, the fabric baby carriers so popular today.

She says it because it's true, but she repeats it to make a point.

In the spot, Motrin linked the sling to back pain, a legitimate way for the brand to strike a chord with new moms. But in an effort to be on mom's sides, the cheeky copy and snarky tone struck out, making the product's user seem self-centered by complaining about backaches from slings.

Though meant to be humorous, the commercial enraged mom bloggers who lashed out and put their own video testimonials on YouTube. The division's vice president posted an apology and, within days, withdrew the spot. In the pre-Internet age, that anger might have amounted to a few nasty letters to the J&J Consumer Info Center; instead the ad incited a public hanging.

If only Motrin had tapped into the Whole Truth that yes, mom's back hurts from carrying a baby, but that pain is a small price for the nurturing value of slings. How could this have been avoided? The ad had all the markings of being written by a junior copywriter pregnant for the first time. A big brand like Motrin should have enlisted a squadron of moms to either contribute to this creative effort or at least vet the copy for a more inclusive tone.

Lessons learned? Women expect both consistency and authenticity from brands they love. Stay true to who you are, even as you court women. The brand was built on a supportive voice, not a sarcastic one. Tread carefully when your brand attempts empathy with Martyrdom. And don't take her complaints at face value. When probed, she'll admit that she actually feels stronger for enduring life's hardships; not to mention, she knows she brings much of her "misery" on herself.

the Whole Truths behind Martyrdom

Ironically, the Whole Truth is that even though a woman might present herself as an overwrought victim, much of her stress is admittedly self-inflicted and she knows it. She's the one who volunteered to organize the carpool. She's the one who filled her calendar with promises.

Women willingly take on most of their to-dos, and given the choice, wouldn't revise the commitments they've made.

Another Whole Truth is that deep down, women believe that without their leadership, nothing would ever get done . . . certainly not well. We've heard women tell stories of their everyday efforts to orchestrate order with families who seem oblivious. One mom told Tracy a story about her family's chronic lateness: "Sometimes I scream, 'Doesn't anyone around here wear a watch? How come I'm the only one who is always watching the clock?'" Tracy asked, "What would happen if you didn't?" The mom looked at her incredulously and then said, with a semi-straight face, "No one would get anywhere on time."

Most marketers wouldn't have poked at what the woman said as Tracy did. But making her recognize that she inflated some of her overwork helped clarify what her Whole Truth really is, which is that she's convinced she does it better than anyone else.

Still, whether it's the pride of female machismo (she can do it all), or her conviction of superiority (no one else can do what she does), some women are unwilling to step away from their self-imposed servitude.

How can a marketer sing her praises to their brand's benefit? **TYSON CHICKEN** tried with a campaign called "Thank You," which wobbled on the tightrope between saluting and insulting overworked moms.

In the TV spots, Tyson featured a mom cooking up an easy meal of chicken pieces, while her kids and husband performed a deadpan, mock tribute. As Dad silently held up his boom box blasting faux Olympic music, the son solemnly thanked Mom. In his next breath, the son suggested that since she'd mastered the quick meal, she'd have more time to help him with his homework. In essence, he was saying, "Thanks, Mom, now do more for me." We haven't seen sales figures on whether this tactic worked, but we'd be shocked if most moms didn't want to club the creative director with a skillet.

Contending with Martyrdom is the trickiest Half Truth. Just talking about Martyrdom and women in the same breath begs for a fight. Indeed, to women, the "martyr" label is an insult. Still, women are quick to jump on the Martyrdom bandwagon, given the chance.

the phenomenon of "out-martyring"

The Half Truth of Martyrdom is so pervasive because it's contagious. Just picture several women standing in line at the supermarket checkout and one woman sighs, "I'm tired." Cue the inevitable chorus

Half Truth:
"I am responsible for everyone and everything."

Whole Truth:
"I take everything on myself because I do it better."

Since she feels that she's the unsung heroine, the marketer's job is to jump on that Whole Truth bandwagon and either reward her for all she's doing, take something annoying off her plate, or make it easier/faster/more fun to do those things she won't let go of.

of "Me, too!" Misery may love company, but sometimes women compete to be the *most* miserable.

If marketers start to ask women about their lives in qualitative research, they're treated to the "out-Martyrdom" phenomenon. As soon as one woman tells her story, she's reflexively out-martyred by others. Marketers who hear multiple women describe hardships and stress, can be misled. What they might not realize is that women pile on for reasons of their own—to wear and share the badge, to be part of the group, to validate their own lives.

Tune into her martyrdom, don't wallow in it.

We saw a great example of this martyr fever at a big retailer event we hosted a few years ago where I moderated an onstage consumer discussion on stress.

One woman on the panel talked about her lack of a boyfriend. Another mom of one ticked through her typical day, starting with a 6:45 a.m. wakeup. Another mentioned a stressful job.

The audience was getting a little restless so I invited questions. Instead, I got speeches. One woman declared, "Let me tell you about *my* typical day. I get up at 5 a.m., I have four kids, two jobs, and more headaches than I can count." Then another: "I want to say to that woman with no boyfriend, I'm sorry, but I'm your age and I have this life-threatening disease" . . . and on and on. What started as feedback escalated to competition.

The women onstage felt one-upped, and the women in the audience dug deeper into their own miseries. When women do this during research, a marketer may assume a higher level of unhappiness than is really true . . . and overreact.

la, la, la, i can't hear you

Another challenge of the Half Truth of Martyrdom is that marketers have a hard time listening to women talk about their stressed lives.

Marketers recoil when women bemoan how busy they are. To many, women's Martyrdom conjures the annoying and unappealing image of a whiner. (And that's not the picture of the customer they want to have.) So often, when we show videos of women mired in Martyrdom, marketers get pulled into their quicksand of complaints. Additionally, this Half Truth of Martyrdom puts marketers, especially male ones on the defensive. We can tell this is happening when male clients start citing all the examples of how in their well-balanced families, men do all the heavy lifting.

Stress is not a contest.

As a marketer, beware of competing with women's stress, especially if she's your customer. As we love to say, "Stress is not a contest." Even if it were, you've got to let your customer win.

help solve her stress

Women can be incredibly empathetic, but they love to play the pity
card, so successful marketers need to base ideas on solving stress
rather than compete with it or amplify it. The first step is getting the
facts, not just the feelings.

To help linen manufacturer **WELSPUN** come up with new concepts
for sheets and bedding, we conducted a sleep survey to understand
women's needs and opportunities. We knew that women everywhere
feel a desperate need for more sleep, but we wanted to discover the
biggest culprit keeping them up at night.

The survey revealed that stress was the leading villain at 54%,
followed by women blaming their nighttime scrolling to-do lists. This
information opened up naming opportunities and even new ways for
fabrics to help fight incessant tossing for more stress-free sleep.

Another marketer, **SEALY POSTUREPEDIC**, was smart enough to
see the opportunity in the stress–sleep war. Rather than harping on
the elusive eight hours of sleep that are so far out of reach, Sealy
promises "Get A Better Six," playing to the Whole Truth of a woman's

dream of even six uninterrupted hours. What woman wouldn't kill for six hours of zzzs? The lesson? Listen to the Whole Truth behind her Half Truth of Martyrdom to learn how you can redefine your product in her terms and you may find you can reposition your current offering into a Whole Truth winner.

A business that's plagued with consumers' stress management is the airline industry, and some brands have navigated this better than others. While both men and women business travelers will trumpet the very true Martyrdom refrain, "I'm so exhausted by business travel," women, especially those with kids waiting at home, take the indignities of travel personally. **CONTINENTAL AIRLINES** was the first to roll out the red carpet at check-in (in their case, it was blue) so that all Elite members, even the straggling latecomers, could bypass the long line of nonmembers. The blue carpet practically shouted, "We know you travel constantly, so here's one annoyance you can take off your plate." They also seem to be the most aggressive about filling any empty business class seat with worthy upgrade candidates, again a life raft for a woman on the edge.

the Whole Truth evolution

The more we've studied this Half Truth, the more we've seen it evolve. Over the last couple of years, we have started to notice another trend. Even the busiest women are finding all kinds of ways to play hooky by either accepting less ambitious goals for themselves or secretly doing fun stuff, like spending hours online under the guise of work.

In research we did for megasite **ABOUT.COM**, women, claiming they are doing research for their families, admitted that they quickly drift into shopping, downloading from iTunes, playing games, posting product reviews, and just zoning out on favorite blogs and sites.

If women are so pressed for time, you'd think surfing the Internet would be squeezed into the scarce wee hours. But though midnight

Half Truth:

"I'm so busy that I have no time for anything else."

Whole Truth:

"I make time for things that I really want to do."

pops for women's online usage, the Whole Truth is she's online all day—at her computer in the office, her BlackBerry in the checkout line, checking her cell when she awakes. Interestingly, moms of young kids, likely the most time-squeezed women, are online the most.

Brands that create escapes for women find that they are only too willing to spend their time and money, when the reason is right. Look at the hours spent posting e-pinions and downloading music. How many women get intoxicated with the craft details on etsy or the product descriptions on eBay? **TRIPADVISOR** is a delicious way to fantasize about potential vacations, and photo websites such as **KODAKGALLERY** have women cataloguing memories like professionals. All these activities take time women are willing to give, no matter how crammed their schedules are. Don't assume that "I'm too busy" means she is. She's only too busy for what's boring or unrewarding.

Internet Usage

Is the Internet an escape from busyness or a cause?
- More than half of all moms are online one to five hours a day.
- More than 36 million moms read or write blogs.

Whole Truths, segmented by stage

Marketers also need to know that all stress is not created equal. And Martyrdom offers all kinds of segmentation opportunities. A young woman may tell you that her schedule of school, work, and social

The Half Truth of Martyrdom can either scare you into just leaving women alone or encourage you to create products and services that ease their stress or help them escape. The choice is yours.

life is just too overwhelming. An Alpha Mom (a media darling who's supposedly maniacally monitoring her family's every move) will tell you that her biggest stress is keeping her highly organized life under control. A boomer woman will tell you she's just weary of putting up with stupid people. Fine-tune the Martyrdom of a segment and you'll find ways to solve it.

For instance, we see a booming market in what we call Beta Moms, women who are doing the best they can with what they have, constantly reshuffling the to-do lists of their lives in order to survive. Her house might not be perfectly clean, but as one woman told us, "The president isn't coming for dinner, so it's all right."

Bestselling books like *Peeing in Peace* and *I Was a Perfect Mom Until I Had Kids* are clarion calls to the millions of women who have decided that good enough has to be good enough. Yes, Beta Mom may sound a lot less camera ready than Alpha Mom, but she's the mother who's the engine of the economy. So marketers have found ways to play to her special brand of Martyrdom.

KFC's "What's for Dinner" campaign managed to transform a bucket of fried chicken into a healthy, nutritious meal option for Beta Moms, despite its superhigh calorie count. The selling point? At least, it's easy

alpha Half Truth:
"I may not be superwoman, but I can be a super mom."

beta Whole Truth:
"I am doing the best I can and that's the best I can do."

and counts as a sit-down hot meal that moms can pick up on the way home from work. With the introduction of Kentucky Grilled Chicken, which surely was designed to appeal to mom's guilt, if not her Good Intentions for lighter fare, KGC for dinner is likely to become a staple. (Oprah offering a coupon for a free KGC meal didn't hurt, either!)

Other marketers capitalizing on making life easier for Beta Moms are **OSCAR MAYER LUNCHABLES** premade lunch kits and **SMUCKERS UNCRUSTABLES** frozen PB&J sandwiches (both successes because they make "easy" easier). And since beverage maker **MOTT'S** knows moms add water to cut the sugar content of juices, they created Motts for Tots, which is essentially juice diluted with water that's "vitamin-fortified" to give Mom a cover for buying it instead of just turning on the tap.

how to avoid the Half Truth of Martyrdom

1. When you invite women to share the difficulties of their stress, try to shut down your personal reactions and focus instead on how you can solve their problems with escape valves and time savers.

2. Humor works, but vet your creative work carefully first with a woman. Don't wallow in a woman's misery, but don't treat it so lightly that she thinks you are making fun of her.

3. Build in a cover story benefit for buying or using your product so that she can keep her martyr badge shiny, even as she buys or enjoys what you're selling.

ego
protection

A few months ago I was shopping for sexy evening shoes, a Rorschach test for any woman's mojo. Ballet flats are practical for everyday, but stilettos keep a woman in the game.

All around me, 20-something shoppers were picking out the most gorgeous and painful-looking styles, while I kept looking for the perfect pair of great but not too high sandals. But suddenly I spotted *them*. I picked up a pair of superhigh, sparkly Stuart Weitzman pumps and asked the balding salesman for them in my size. (I only mention "balding" to give you a heads up where this is headed.)

He brought them out and I slipped them on (or rather tried to stuff my toes inside) and gingerly stepped to the mirror, feeling not quite like a Vegas showgirl but darn close. I asked casually if he had the next bigger size and he said no. But I was smitten, and I couldn't take them off. I said to him, "Maybe I can make these work." And he looked at me, shook his head, and whispered, "When you get to be *our* age, you don't do dumb things the second time around. You need to order a bigger size."

Our age? *Second* time around? But I'm only . . . !

Somehow the shoes had lost their shine.

Ego-shattering moments lurk just around the bend for women of every age and at every stage of life, like being asked when you're due when you're not even pregnant, or being called "ma'am" for the first time (yes, we know it's a courtesy but not when you're only 32).

In everyday life, women dodge the slings and arrows hurled their way in the form of left-handed compliments or unintended disrespect. It's bad enough when a teen son rejects his mom's friend request on Facebook; it's unforgiveable when women feel dissed or underestimated by the products they buy and the people they buy from. So it's not surprising that women adopt the coping mechanism of Ego Protection, the fourth Half Truth, to shore up their best beliefs about who they are.

believing her own Half Truth

This Half Truth of Ego Protection is pervasive and addictive. Some women will repeat their alter-ego stories so often that they begin to believe them. Their Half Truths become kind of überwishful thinking that's deeply internalized and believed.

Why does this matter to marketers? If you're a technology marketer and your prospective customer presents herself in research as a "techie" but hasn't even taken her new digital camera out of the box, and you tailor your new high-tech toy for her maximum utility, prepare for a sales shortfall. If she walks into your auto dealership with her midlife ego starving for a sexy convertible and you steer her toward the sedans, prepare to meet her wrath. (One 60-plus woman told us that she was in the market for a sporty two-seater, one seat for her, and the other for her purse.) Unfortunately for marketers, women become artful dodgers when their ego is threatened, and public exposure in research or at the counter is just that kind of threat.

meet the real women inside

As a marketer, you need to know that you are marketing to at least two women with every *one* you sell to—the woman you see and the woman you don't.

What we've observed from a decade of interviewing women is that many have adopted what Sigmund Freud first identified as the "ego-ideal" (or in our words, the idealized ego), a perfected version of themselves, their talents, or personalities, even when untrue. Dr. Freud traced the roots of this idealized self to childhood narcissism, where, as young girls, women yearned to be seen as perfect in their parents' eyes. As adults, and perhaps under the glare of a marketer's microscope or the scrutiny of other authority figures, women protect that idealized ego as the expression of their best (happier, smarter, prettier, younger) self. Their endgame might be being loved, admired, or just recognized as special by those they respect or fear.

Women present themselves as whom they choose to be, depending on circumstances, and channel the persona that works for them. Sometimes those personalities have been nurtured for years, other times they are just responses to the issue at hand. At the parent–teacher conference, the working woman wants to be taken seriously as a dedicated mom, so she dresses casually and stashes her BlackBerry inside her purse. The 50-something mother of the bride tells the bridal shop owner that she's content with whatever simple dress doesn't outshine her daughter's, but inwardly sees herself making her big entrance to the ensuing gasps of "Wow! She *can't* be the mother!" Today's new grandmothers have taken to refusing the "Grandma" moniker, asking for "Glamma" or their first names instead.

As a marketer, you need to know you are marketing to at least two women with every one you sell to—the woman you see and the woman you don't.

These assumed or hidden identities are really a form of Ego Protection, a way for women to shield their fears and promote their inner hopes by crafting a self-image for the outside world. Marketers might be surprised at who's inside.

For example, a financial service advisor may assume he's selling securities to a successful careerist, who's prepared to make a deal. But the astute broker might notice that she's dragging her feet on the decision. Why? Inside, that same woman may be an anxious and skeptical worrier who's suffering from bag lady syndrome, fearful that she will lose all her money one day and turn to selling apples on the corner.

The wealth management group of **US TRUST** hit this dual personality nail on the head with a commercial that showed a confident businesswoman and described her this way: "She owns a villa in St. Barths, a condo in Sun Valley . . . yet a part of her still lives in a cul de sac in (smalltown) Ohio." The bank recognized that even a financial highflier can be a conservative investor. Only by reading her right on the outside can you get the chance to mine the deeper, more profound insights within.

It is interesting that the current economic downturn is breeding a new kind of Ego Protection, where even someone who could afford to chill in St. Barth's will proclaim they're staycationing instead, to show prudence and avoid the whiff of wastefulness.

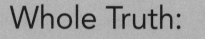

marketer's ego check

Maybe marketers get fooled by this Half Truth because they're caught up in an Ego Protection game of their own. Examine the profile of your target customer in your brand strategy. We get a kick out of how many ad agencies describe their client's ideal customer as . . . ideal. Let's face it. We're not going to hear this descriptor: She's an overweight, undisciplined woman with a poor self-image and a big dose of resentment toward skinny people. (But wouldn't approaching the project from this angle encourage the most amazing creative work?!)

A more typical strategy is the figment of an agency's aspirations: "Our customer is young, attractive, fashionable, has a good sense of style and humor and a Portuguese Water Spaniel, likes to Tweet while eating Pinkberry, and has an active social life."

With one retail client, we recruited women **She's NOT** based on their own store's credit card reports, so **our customer!** we knew they were the brand's legitimate high spenders. Yet the retailer was so uncomfortable being confronted with the "wrong women" who didn't fit their idealized customer image that we actually posted annual product spend under each woman's photograph in our report to help underline the truth.

Your own Ego Protection can undermine your business success. If you can't love your brand for what it is and who it's for, then it's time to shove your ego and your résumé out the door.

branding her ego

The most obvious place where ego comes in to play in marketing is in the most aspirational brand names, particularly those designer names that function as badges. In those categories, which are conspicuous when used or worn, your product itself is a surrogate for a woman's ego. It's not new news that a designer label adds ego cachet.

The ego play of designer names or expert celebrities at mass-retail features a parade of Martha Stewart, Emeril Lagasse, and Rachel Ray, who are marketed across media, from product to in-store appearances to ads. Their success plays to the truth that women may pretend not to care about endorsements, but they really do. But how can a marketer know when a woman's telling the truth about whether a designer works for your brand?

One way is to be sure she knows whose name she's dropping. For one project, we were so convinced that women were exaggerating just how much they really knew some designer names that we tucked in a fictitious brand between Donna Karan and Calvin Klein in our list of names to check off as labels they owned. Check, check, check! So much for their label expertise!

Another test is the "coffee test." When you research a series of potential designers or celebrities to endorse a brand, ask women, "Which of these women would you like to meet for a cup of coffee?" It's a great way to weed out the names of celebrities who might be ego inflators but are actually perceived as frenemies.

is she green or . . . green-ish?

Thanks to the strength of their convictions, women often make marketers think trends are bigger than they are. The green trend, for example, is a case of women being selectively honest. Women will spout their green credentials effortlessly because it presents them as more conscientious consumers. "I only buy organic." "My home is healthier because of green products." Saying you're exclusively green or that you are scrupulously earth conscious is accurate for some, but we have found it's claimed more often than

Is she as squeaky green as she claims to be?

it's true. Women know that green is good and waste is bad, so after adopting a green behavior or two, they will start to talk as if they're actually growing their dinner and recycling the plates, even if their only green gesture is a bottle of Method tile spray in the shower.

A way to judge the degree of Ego Protection is to listen to not only what she *says* she cares about but also how *confidently* she asserts what she says to others.

While the green trend is huge and obviously not retreating, we think that marketers who buy all of women's protestations of perfection in this area could lose their shirts. Note how the economy is affecting the more discretionary green buying. Look at the Rodale magazine *Organic Style*. Actually you can't read it now because it failed, yet it was a clearly targeted magazine, well-researched and before it's time, intended to help women make the decisions they claim to be so important. The magazine teetered between her Half Truth, "I want to be as green as I can be," and her Whole Truth, "I'll go green as long as it still tastes good, looks pretty, and doesn't cost more." Green, organic, natural, locally grown, no matter what the language, intent to purchase is often overturned when pricing comes

PROTESTING TOO MUCH

Jen cracked up at her own comment while interviewing moms about baby apparel and supplies. One mom killed every idea with her principle of buying only natural products. She knocked down concept after concept for not being squeaky green. In exasperation, as the woman nixed a baby bottle carrier made of sturdy and safe BPA-free plastics, Jen said, "Okay, would you like it if I said it was made of hemp?!"

up. Our take on the Whole Truth? She's "green-ish" and can be more practical than purist.

In work we did on towels, women were excited about a bamboo eco-towel that promised to dry faster in the dryer. Women liked it all right, but their reason was more practical (and selfish!): "I want it to dry *me* faster, and I want it to dry fast on the rack, so that it doesn't get rank and I don't have to wash it as often." What was that about the earth-sustaining bamboo?

We don't mean to underestimate the power of the green movement and the growing number of consumers who try to make choices that sustain the planet. Niche, squeaky green brands like **SEVENTH GENERATION** have penetrated the cleaning aisles of the biggest chains. But mass brands like **CLOROX GREENWORKS** cleaned up by offering a dose of feel-good green clean with the silent but mighty hero name of Clorox to assure germ killing. By securing the imprimatur of the Sierra Club and others, the brand has managed to tread the narrow line between green and effective. And we've heard that many women are displaying their Greenworks products on their countertops, a giveaway to their badge value.

Women are still figuring out their green ground rules. Be careful that you don't assume that the green game she talks will end up as cash in the register at the end of the day.

playing to her undercover ego

Women lying about their age to strangers is a running joke. But why would a woman conceal the truth about her appearance from people she loves? Often, she's guarding her idealized self-image. But if she's not telling her significant other a key truth, how can you expect her to tell it to you? (One in seven women buy a bridal gown one or more sizes smaller than they wear.)

Half Truth:
"I want to be as green as I can be."

Whole Truth:
"I'll go green as long as it still tastes good/looks pretty and doesn't cost more."

We like to ask questions that unveil the hidden ego. In a beauty session, we asked women to describe themselves three ways: "What age are you? What age do you feel inside? And what age do people take you for?" The first question was answered accurately. The second answer always drew on her humor: "I'm either 30 or I'm 80. Nothing in between!"

But the third question was the most revealing of her Ego Protection because that's where she was able to admit what she was feeling inside, using her perceptions of others' assessments. Women bragged about being carded or being hit on by younger men. This bravado may be a cover for their Whole Truth that compliments may be harder to come by so they concoct their own. A brand that recognizes that women's fragile egos need a mental hug every once in a while wins.

For years, **EILEEN FISHER** apparel has catered to aging egos with her high-fashion sensibility. Midlife women constantly complain there are no clothes that fit their changing bodies and their only choices are baggy or matronly. Most fashion marketers avoid even showing imagery of older women, for fear of bruising their own youth-obsessed egos!

Eileen Fisher hit on the perfect lifestyle and psychic imagery with a campaign featuring beautiful women, many of them graying, fit but not stick-thin, and most of all happy in their gracefully ageless outfits instead of screaming "This comes with elastic waistbands and an AARP card in the pocket!"

In addition to branding products to convey that you understand women's ego frustrations, it's also key to include features that will pay off your promise. **NOT YOUR DAUGHTER'S JEANS** is a great example of this. The brand understands that women are mocked by their teen daughters for wearing high-waisted, boring "mom jeans" yet are freaked at the idea of muffin-top midriffs over low-cut, skin-tight teen jeans. The jeans, with just enough lycra and edgy attitude, do such a good job connecting with women in a fashionable and comfortable way that they command a price that her ego will happily pay.

Age and appearance issues can stretch beyond fashion and cosmetics into unlikely areas such as healthcare. We were retained by a pharmaceutical company to figure out the barriers to women's interest in hormone therapy. The obvious answers were related to widespread negative media reports and highly publicized product trials. Yet even as those results were mitigated or overturned, women still resisted the drugs. By Power Listening, we discovered that Ego Protection turned out to be the unseen culprit when one 50-year-old admitted that she didn't want to investigate her nagging hot flashes because if her younger husband found out she was menopausal, he'd think she was old.

Why does a marketer care if a woman hides the truth from her husband? In the case of the menopausal patient, marketers need to realize that the barrier to usage can be more than a lack of information or a fear of drug side-effects; her ego faced the block of her own mortality or the risk of losing her appeal. Messaging that helps her see herself as young enough (rather than old enough!) for this product would connect.

protect her ego with stealth products

In the area of product development, it's important to adapt to the workings of her "idealized ego." Note that her idealized ego is not to be confused with her aspirations. Aspirations are what she dreams of being. Her idealized ego is the composite of who she presents herself as in everyday life. And you've got to observe her in everyday life and conversation to find those loopholes. If she never wears her reading glasses, that's a sign that she's in age denial.

Rather than force women to expose their assumed identities, smart marketers find ways to sneak past women's resistance and fulfill their needs with products that include stealth features.

The **JITTERBUG** phone was invented as an antidote to cell phones with tiny keypads and superfeatures that are de rigueur for younger people. The Jitterbug features large keys, simple features, even the ability to use voice commands for frequently used numbers. While the phone is marketed for older folks with visual limitations or technophobia, many younger consumers have taken a shine to a cell that's a no-brainer and requires no reading glasses to read.

Likewise, **AMAZON'S KINDLE** has a benefit that will be instantly understandable to most boomers: all the downloaded books can be read in the font size you prefer. Though most boomer readers aren't ready to be caught reading large-print books on a bus, a flick of a button on the Kindle allows readers to change the font size undetected by others. The ego remains protected!

Apparel sizing is another ego killer that puts a woman's vital statistics right out on the selling floor. Apparel maker **CHICO'S** brilliantly challenged the traditions of women's sizing that forced any larger women into high double digits. Chico's recognized that women, when not at their ideal weights, didn't want to be relegated to the muumuu ghetto. At Chico's, women are a size one, two, or

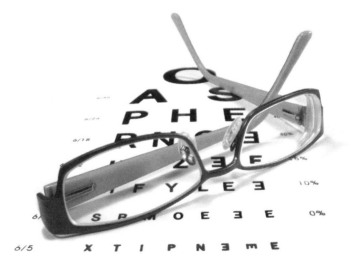

three, that's it. Their egos are intact, as are those of millions of like-minded Chico's aficionados.

bracing for her ego revenge

What's fascinating about a woman's Ego Protection is that she may stew silently until she hits a boiling point with marketers and sales-people that blows her cover. Women, who may be mild or diplomatic under most circumstances, will whip out their evil twin when it's time to duel with errant sales and service people.

When we've asked women to describe their identities as shop-pers, they are proud to claim their power. As one woman told us, "I'm a 'you've got one chance to screw up' shopper."

Another woman we interviewed demonstrated her revenge tech-nique on a salesman who made her feel he was too busy to take her call. In what was clearly an oft-repeated performance, she mimicked her best imperious voice, as she raved at the hapless receptionist, "You tell your boss, this is an *escalated* phone call, use that *word* and tell him *I want service right now!*" As the other women in the group applauded, I could see her relax into the knowl-edge that this story only got better with the tell-ing, securing her place as queen of customer service revenge.

> I'm a you've-got-one-chance-to-screw-up shopper!

Marketers of services faced with an irate customer like this can figure out whether her anger is real or manufactured by starting with the magic words, "You're right. Now, how can I make this better for you?" Play to her ego; all she's really wanting is the respect she deserves—and to not be seen as the cowering, customer chump.

In the car business, moms will say that one of the toughest rites of passage is the moment they are faced with the inevitable minivan

MINIVAN **REVENGE**

Jen adds this dose of Whole Truth revenge to a mini-van purchase: The birth of my twins and an exodus from the city to the 'burbs turned my life upside down. But it was buying a minivan that nearly killed me. I went to the **HONDA** dealer kicking and screaming, but the choice was out of my hands. If we wanted the infant car seats to fit in the car and have room for a spare adult, we had to take the plunge. I was floating in the air looking down on someone else's life. How could I drive it and still hold my head up high? But my husband and I bought a loaded Odyssey and I immediately tried to protect my ego. I even coined a new acronym (MUV, multiuse vehicle) so we wouldn't have to utter the word minivan. It didn't stick. I decided the only way I was going to teach this minivan a lesson was if the first time I drove it, I wore stilettos. After the inaugural ride, I felt much better. And since then, I've even driven it in my pajamas.

decision. As much as women will try to stall or delay, the arrival of multiple little ones and their friends forces the minivan moment.

Rather than try to talk women out of their minivan resentment, **VOLKSWAGEN** turned the tables with a humorous campaign featuring Brooke Shields. In one spot, she deadpans, "There's an epidemic sweeping our nation. Women everywhere are having babies just to get the Volkswagen Routan. Have a baby for love, not for German engineering." In an online long-form ad, she fronts a mockumentary that shows how the baby boom is really an excuse to allow parents to buy the Routan. Brooke literally switches the irritation of minivan revenge to unbridled minivan desire. This creative jujitsu is a genius way to anticipate and understand her Ego Protection and convert it to your brand's advantage.

detecting her ego trap

One area where women are superguarded about their egos is with luxury or higher-priced purchases. Outing their true identity requires some clever espionage. We once asked women who claimed they were luxury shoppers to bring their favorite shoes to a department store's research session. Funny how the lower priced, scuffed-up "comfort brands" dominated the room! (Maybe the Manolos inspired their visits, but Naturalizers filled their closets.)

Cosmetics usage is another mixed bag. Most women use a mix of expensive and cheaper brands, but will name-drop the fancier products when they are with other women. Worse, they will tell an online survey that they exclusively use brands that they may have only tried once. Ask a woman to empty her purse on the spot. If she says she only wears department store cosmetics, see what falls out onto her lap—Vaseline lip balm or Chanel gloss?

In our conversations with women, they are more open with us than with most other people. Sometimes, they don't have to open their purses, or their jackets! In sessions we did discussing the meaning of femininity, one woman in work boots and jeans literally pulled back her EMS uniform to reveal her "hoochie bra," as she called it, the symbol of who she really was inside.

If you're not quite that personal with your customers, then ask them to bring something to your research session that might reveal a truth that she may be hiding. When doing work for **SPECIAL K**, we asked women to bring clothes that didn't fit any longer but that they were still hoping to wear and couldn't bear to toss. Women brought dresses three sizes too small, jeans lingering from college days, all garments that spoke to their true identities. Both the sizes and the sexier styling of those lost outfits taught us about their aspirations, as well as how far they'd go to fit into them again.

We were most amazed at how convinced each woman was that inside she was still the woman who was sexier or younger than the woman sitting before us. While it's tempting to respond to this situation with "we love you the way you are" advertising, the Whole Truth is that women see themselves as their better selves. That's why Special K, an extraordinarily successful brand, continues to hold out the hope of the tight jeans or the slinky red dress, even if they are a few pounds beyond that. Market to the truth in *her* mirror, that's what she's buying.

how to avoid the Half Truth of Ego Protection

1. Remember each woman harbors some degree of Ego Protection and may be describing her ideal self to you rather than her real self. Try on-the-spot surprise questions to keep her "perfect script" at bay.

2. Taking her ideal ego seriously does not mean being serious. Humor is one of the best ways to be frontal about what she's hiding inside.

3. Zigging when competitors zag can help you own a woman's unspoken fantasies better than conforming to category norms.

secret keeping

ormer supermodel Tyra Banks, enraged by media criticism of her extra pounds, walked onto the set of her TV talk show, wearing a red swimsuit and a sign that read "160," her weight, in defiant, giant numbers. Surprise! The entire studio audience did the same.

Teenage girls email naked self-portraits to high school boyfriends and sadly, the entire class gets a peek.

New moms describe every detail of labor on their blogs and post videos of every one of their child's burps and bumps on YouTube for millions to share.

Do women really keep secrets anymore? In this culture of confession, with Oprah as high priestess, why would anyone keep a secret when telling them is so easy? In a real-time, digital, Twitter world, where every private thought can be broadcast in a split second, Are today's women just more calculating about what they reveal and what they conceal? How many women post their most flattering (if out of date) pictures on Facebook? Ever read someone's supposedly accurate profile on Match.com?

The Whole Truth is that women share those secrets, online and off, that portray them the way they like to be perceived and support the personalities they aspire to. Conversely, they safeguard the secrets that damage that image.

Secrets don't have to be damaging. They can be "little white secrets." Ask a beauty marketer how many women play down their sins of self-inflicted sun damage while bragging that they wear SPFs all the time. Ask a pharmaceutical marketer how many female consumers promise compliance, yet double down on dosage based on their own doctoring. Ask a furniture marketer how many women claim to have modern, simple taste, yet actually fill their houses with overstuffed furniture and knickknack collections?

You say you don't keep secrets? Is there a small blip on your resume that seems to have been deleted? Was there an event in your life you've never confessed to your spouse? Ever eat a cookie in the bathroom? Keeping secrets is something we learn to do when we are as young as three or four years old. Holding some things inside is part of human nature.

So if you think women don't keep secrets from you, you're in for an awakening. We've certainly exposed more than our share of them.

why she hides

While this entire book dissects those Half Truths that women tell you, this chapter will take on those secrets that are conscious. Secret Keeping is the collection of deliberate behaviors motivated by women's deeper reasons to hide: shame, embarrassment, pride, self-delusion, and fear. Her Secret Keeping can be a means of preserving denial, of withholding trust, or of safe-guarding personal relationships from prying eyes. And sometimes, Secret Keeping is just her private way of telling the world, "None of your business!"

When Secret Keeping squelches key information you need to know, it can undermine your plans in a big way. Some marketers have nonetheless figured out how to crack the code, but many others are unknowingly in the dark, wondering why she's not buying or believing what their brands have to say. This chapter should turn on the light.

Why do women keep secrets from others and from the marketers who want their business? Naturally, the reasons vary depending on how big the secret, but here are a few we've noticed. We'll start with the more innocent ones and work up to the serious whoppers.

secrets she proudly hides or flaunts

Some secrets are meant to be shared, as social currency. Women love the idea of a secret because it bestows credibility and insider power on the teller and then when she spreads the word, she blesses the "tell-ee" as a co-conspirator. The fashion industry understands this idea of a fascinating game of "insider" deception. An example is a brand like **ZARA**, exploding globally thanks to the company's talent for quickly adapting designer trends into more accessibly priced apparel. It's both a best-kept insider's secret and a bragging point for women.

She gets to decide whether to squirrel away the price tag or flash it as social currency among like-minded friends.

In a tight economy, keeping shopping secrets is becoming an Olympic sport for higher income women who feel compelled to hide whatever they spend rather than appear shallow. The frugal rich are finding themselves shipping purchases rather than being seen toting designer bags while others scrimp and bargain shop.

We've come a long way from hair coloring that "only your hairdresser knows for sure" to bragging about how we've whitened our teeth, injected our lines, or pumped up body parts. Know whether your brand is a secret she wants to keep or one she'll proudly broadcast.

chagrined into silence

Secrets about small transgressions or life's everyday mistakes keep brand marketers from getting at a woman's Whole Truth. Sometimes her smallest "bad" behaviors will loom large in a woman's mind and she'll block your access. Will she tell you how many hours she really spent downloading music instead of organizing her home office? Did she really convince the kids to clean their rooms as promised or did she do it herself because she does it better and faster? Sometimes these small secrets make the difference in a creative strategy.

For example, while women today like to refer to their homes as "comfortable" and aren't that worked up about housekeeping faux pas, they do feel some of the blame when things aren't up to snuff.

Successful brands fix the small mistakes so that there's no emotional blowback on women. Bounty's new campaign "Bring It" recently veered from years of focusing on the annoyance of kids' spills to moms treating accidents as nonevents. Likewise, products that provide instant amnesty, like Procter & Gamble's **TIDE-TO-GO**, **MR. CLEAN MAGIC ERASER**, or **FEBREZE**, get rid of life's small embarrassments so that women don't even have to try to hide the stains or smudges or smells that give away spotty cleaning habits. It's not that women won't divulge these "secret" problems, it's that they will downplay their importance

because they're bothered that they reflect on them, even when it's not their fault.

Some products are actually designed to guard her secrets of chagrin, like **SPANX**, the booming "foundation" garment brand. Spanx has built an entire business out of hiding unwanted bumps, lumps, and cellulite. Women know that they can get away with a few extra pounds if they're wearing this highly elastic underwear. The brand was pretty undercover until actress Gwyneth Paltrow appeared on Oprah, just weeks after giving birth, and confessed that she was wearing two pairs of Spanx to fit into her skirt. Instant bragging rights for a secret!

Are there other marketing opportunities in these chagrin-inducing secrets? Case in point: women might not like to confess that they spend many hours online at work, researching travel plans or playing poker. By getting her to come clean about when and where she's online (without marking her as a slacker!), advertisers can discover her attention apertures, no matter what time of day. That's why brands from **POTTERY BARN** to **J.CREW** pop-up online all day long to attract the deskbound shopper. As one working woman said to us, "I'd rather order it online and wait for it than waste my lunch hour in line at the Gap with the locusts at the mall waiting for that same black turtleneck."

One thing to remember about these small chagrin-inducing secrets is that you shouldn't rub them in. While advertisers are long past the annoying "Ring around the collar" harangues of **WISK** laundry detergent, there are still examples of companies who seem to think it's funny to show women having to deal with the grime of life. Give women a break! Make the dirt fun, like the **SWIFFER** campaign that humorously shows a woman's old-fashioned but ineffective mop begging to get her back, like a rejected boyfriend. That's putting chagrin where it belongs . . . behind her.

silent pride and embarrassment

When a woman harbors a secret that is tied deeply to her feelings of either failure or disappointing others, she's hiding secrets of shame. These are the kind of secrets that keep healthcare marketers up at night. For instance, from an early age, women are expected and wired to be strong guardians of their families and loved ones. But when their own illness compromises their caretaking, women will try to keep symptoms secret to avoid "wasting time" going to the doctor or getting a prescription. The Whole Truth? Women are often too proud to say that they're scared and too embarrassed to admit they need help. How can you sell a cure to someone who's hiding out?

For instance, incontinence sufferers mask a problem that is just too publicly embarrassing to share aloud. Women are willing to laugh about the occasional leak when they sneeze but shy away from acknowledging the hugely restrictive effect of serious incontinence, like having to mentally map where every restroom is or stashing extra underwear in their glove compartments. So they withhold the gory details, not just from marketers, but also from doctors and family members.

Ethnography is a great way to get at what's too embarrassing for group discussion. Tracy filmed a woman with incontinence who shared her system for back-up bed linens and another who confessed the toll the problem was taking on her marriage. That video was helpful to the creative teams developing the messaging, as well as for their audience of doctors, who needed a dose of women's reality to up their own empathy levels and interviewing techniques.

And how can a marketer create advertising to appeal to a woman when she squirms at even the mention of your product? Finding ways through humor or new language or stealth marketing is often an answer.

Half Truth:
"I don't really have a big problem so I keep it to myself."
Whole Truth:
"I know everyone knows but I pretend they don't."

Some brands creatively cope with embarrassing secrets. **ATTENDS** Healthcare products are shipped from **WALGREENS'** online pharmacy in discreet packaging so customers don't have to be red faced with the delivery guy. **WOMEN'S TYLENOL** Menstrual Relief, which we named, purposely packaged itself in purple so that husbands sent out on menstrual reconnaissance missions at night could just grab the "purple one" and not make a mistake.

Secret Keeping is not only a mom or boomer issue. Young women have been known to keep secrets from their doctors on everything from sexual activity to drinking and smoking to avoid reprimands or embarrassment. And doctors play the secret avoiders when they don't want to deal with a long conversation about sex in their 15 minutes of patient time.

While it's an easy laugh to see women trying not to be seen buying a pregnancy kit in a drugstore, more marketers in the feminine categories would be wise to help her keep a little dignity in the aisle, or the "pink ghetto" as Jen calls it. Perhaps the best efforts belong to **TAMPAX**, who've taken a cue from younger women's comfort with "down there" and lightened up the tone of the category with commercials that brought tampons front and center, like using one to stop a leak in a rowboat on a date, so that no one needs to feel weird in the drugstore aisle.

protecting self-delusion

Women will purposely keep some secrets from you as a way to keep themselves in a blissful state of denial. Smoking cessation is a category where this is chronic.

When Jen was interviewing women who had registered as smokers in advance, she was surprised when several said they didn't smoke. "But you are a smoker, aren't you?" she asked. One woman answered, "No,

Half Truth:
"I'm not really a smoker."

Whole Truth:
"I bum them from friends so it doesn't count."

I'm not a smoker because I don't buy cigarettes. I just bum them from my girlfriends after work."

Several other women agreed with that same train of thought, hiding their secret for such a long time that they denied the behavior they were actually doing.

Marketers who contend with serious Secret Keeping would be well advised to put themselves personally into the dialogue. To put one group at ease, Jen admitted that she herself had smoked, which not only opened them up but let them know that there was no fooling someone who'd clearly been there.

The women, so committed to concealing their habit, demonstrated the inconvenient and extreme lengths of Secret Keeping. One respondent drove a mile away from her office parking lot to catch a smoke on break. A mom said she only smoked in the backyard so her kids couldn't see. Anyone who's ever loved a smoker knows the smell lingers no matter how much mouthwash or fragrance is involved, and yet mature women had such a deep need to preserve their secret that they believed they weren't getting caught.

By refusing to disclose these delusional secrets, women keep the truth from being real or inviting the displeasure of others, as if denying the secret makes it untrue.

Imagine how much this Secret Keeping limited the potential target audience for smoking-cessation products that would "out" women's habit. That's why **NICODERM** patches come in clear instead of just beige bandage colors, and **COMMIT** gum could pass for a blister pack of Trident to hide the cure that would give away the habit.

How can a marketer sell women a product that solves a problem they won't admit they even have? **GLAXOSMITHKLINE** took an interesting tack when, rather than present the obvious and well-known cancer dangers of smoking, they took a backdoor approach by connecting smoking to aging skin. It's a fact that smokers get a grayish tinge to their skin, lines around their mouths from the puffing action, and premature, deep facial lines. By presenting Commit as a product that could slow, even reverse, the aging signs from smoking, marketers made women take notice.

When a woman is in denial, the burden is on the marketer to search for language, imagery, and benefits that she's willing to talk about. Call it camouflage marketing, but it works.

the pain of shame

The "worst" kind of secrets women keep are likely those that relate to something as serious as contending with addiction or a past trauma. The toll of guarding this kind of secret weighs heavy on a woman's heart, but the risk of confessing comes at too high a price.

Marketers in the public service space grapple with this all the time. Several years ago, in order to help create sensitive public service messaging for victims of domestic abuse, **LIFETIME TELEVISION** assigned us to figure out the right words to use to connect with abused women.

We proceeded very, very carefully. Though we'd assembled prior abuse victims, at first, none even acknowledged it. We recognized that only by Power Listening, slowly letting women tell their stories, at their pace and timing, could we learn what we needed to know.

A technique I used in that situation was to share my own story, not of abuse but of receiving frightening, anonymous phone calls. That was a way to remove the stigma that it was "their" problem and create a safe haven that encouraged a brave woman to share her story, which inspired others to follow.

Half Truth:
"I feel too awful to admit that I am in this situation."
Whole Truth:
"Because I can't tell anyone, I feel so alone."

The **PARTNERSHIP FOR A DRUG-FREE AMERICA** organization wanted to probe the mindset of moms troubled by their kid's early drug experimentation. At first, women were in a state of "not my kid" denial, despite the fact that prior to the sessions they had all admitted that their kids had problems.

Tracy worried that the one outspoken mom felt suddenly exposed as the lone truth teller in the group. Tracy said, "Everyone in this room is in a similar situation. Don't feel that you're the only one. We can all learn from each other." By normalizing something shameful, Tracy was able to get other women to share the information we needed to help the Partnership.

Women will hide secrets of shame from those who come across as judges rather than as counselors and commiserators. Secret Keeping calls for a big dose of humanity, empathy, and unabashed candor. If you don't feel it, hire it.

marketers' secrets put her on guard

But how about the secrets you keep from her? You might examine your own conscience as to whether your own behavior is contributing to distrust that makes her reluctant to divulge things to you specifically and marketers in general. Hidden fees for credit cards, magazine subscriptions that trap her with automatic renewal, pricing that disguises hidden costs, punitive return policies, and downsized products all are culprits in their own way. While her Secret Keeping annoys you, consider how many marketers and retailers have kept the truth from her. No wonder she's got a few secrets of her own.

Building a brand that welcomes the truth, stands behind its products, and creates a two-way dialogue at every touch point gives you a better chance of being the one she'll trust with her Whole Truth.

Interestingly, some of the big private-label brands from chains such as supermarket **PUBLIX** and mass-market **TARGET** are gaining share because it's clear that consumers aren't paying for marketing expenses like advertising and fancy packaging. It's not necessary to be "plain" to show you're not a secret-hoarding brand, but being plainspoken is a step in the right direction.

the benefits of unearthing secrets

This section may have scared you a little into thinking that there are secrets you could never unveil. We thought that too, at first. When we set out to build Just Ask a Woman, we didn't plan to morph from marketers to therapists for thousands of women (and funnily enough, sometimes for our clients, too). But that's exactly what happened. We really didn't realize the power of what happens when our more personal and probing techniques spur women to reveal the deeper secrets they hide. In nearly every one of our hundreds of group sessions, there is always at least one huge a-ha moment among the women. And the reward for telling a secret within a supportive atmosphere is a kind of therapy in itself, thanks to the tips they learn from other women.

In one healthcare research session, a woman suffering from the brain fog of fibromyalgia sat with tears running down her face, clutching a handmade calendar that she carried to keep track of

what day it was. When we asked about it, she whispered that she had two or three duplicates placed around the house in case she lost one. With that startling revelation, four other women raised their hands to confess that they too were often "lost." Suddenly, the symptom of disorientation was verified and clarified in a very human way for the brand.

So often in our work, women will applaud each other for coming out for the first time about a shared but unspoken problem. And our sponsoring brands get the credit for providing the truth-telling environment. So, while we aren't trained psychologists or counselors, somehow we have grown to be brand therapists and that's what's driven our success and our clients'.

how to avoid the Half Truth of Secret Keeping

1. Her secrets can actually work to your advantage if your brand can tap into the "best-kept secret" brand territory. Ask her if your brand has bragging rights.

2. To get her to open up her deeper secrets to you, prepare to do the same with her. A woman will trust the marketers who are unafraid of showing their own vulnerabilities.

3. If she's got a secret that's standing between your brand and success, you may have to employ stealth techniques, like affinity groups of friends who will force her to tell her truth even if she resists. Remember, the best marketers need this truth to do right by her, not to be busybodies!

the five
Half Truths
at retail

N ow that you've got a grip on the five Half Truths that can give your marketing plans a run for the money, let's look at how all of them come to play at retail. Here's where the GAMES of Good Intentions, Approval Seeking, Martyrdom, Ego Protection, and Secret Keeping can surprise you.

Even the most insightful strategies and the most innovative products can fail at the moment of sale. At every touch point, from presentation and store environment to customer service and loyalty programs to checkout and returns, the realities of retail can either deliver a brand marketer's hopes or dash them.

To women, marketing is retail. They don't know or think about the hard work of brand managers, product developers, and ad agency–types. They don't care about the things you agonize over. They are much more interested in where they buy, how they're treated, and what kind of value they get. And they define the buying experience broadly, including online, on the phone, in the catalog, from the agent, in the showroom, and yes, in the store.

In marketing circles, the buying decision has come to be called "the moment of truth" but is that moment built on women's Half Truths or Whole Truths? This case will truth-detect the two giants of mass retailing—**WAL-MART**, retail's biggest player, and **TARGET**, their closest competitor—to determine which is tapping into a woman's Whole Truth and which is stuck in the Half Truth zone, and how both are dealing with her G-A-M-E-S.

the truth about Wal-Mart

There is hardly a major product marketer who shouldn't thank his or her lucky stars for Wal-Mart. Wal-Mart is the 8-million-pound gorilla that's both respected and feared for its huge leverage over so many suppliers' fates through its hard-knuckled price negotiations.

Though the brand has been plagued with criticism for its faults (crowded aisles, dowdy clothes, lowbrow image), the fact is that its low prices entice women to shop there more than anywhere else. Since the proof of a woman's retail Whole Truth isn't just what she says but where she actually buys, Wal-Mart is a Whole Truth brand, hands down.

Tight economic times play to Wal-Mart's success. This is true not only because of the company's lowest-price philosophy, but because the chain is now able to reap the fruit of years of renovation and policy change. Newer stores with more organized layouts, better customer service, prolific grocery selection, low-priced prescriptions, and well-stocked electronics at phenomenal prices meet most consumers' demands. And yet, if asked, "Which is the Whole Truth brand, Wal-Mart or Target?" most marketers would probably still answer "Target." Why?

For years, the inner circles of ad agencies and marketing insiders loved to bash Wal-Mart and worship Target. Pick a battle, from employee discrimination to environmental impact of new stores,

Half Truth:
"I don't go to Wal-Mart because it's too crowded/ chaotic/ downscale."

Whole Truth:
"I'm a closet Wal-Mart shopper because the prices are right."

and marketing cognoscenti, Wall Street analysts, and major media piled on Wal-Mart as the enemy. Marketers were guilty of their own Half Truths of Ego Protection of status ("I'd never shop there") and Approval Seeking among peers ("Isn't it awful how little they pay their people?"). Bashing Wal-Mart while fawning over Target's cool factor seemed to be a common way of asserting one's hipness, political correctness, and high-minded superiority.

Women, while putting more of their dollars into Wal-Mart's registers, held their own negative images of the retailer. Although millions turned to Wal-Mart for groceries and household basics for kids,

	Half Truth	Whole Truth
Good Intentions	I want to save money so I shop Wal-Mart.	Wal-Mart is okay for food and kid's stuff, but I would rather splurge on myself somewhere else.
Martyrdom	Wal-Mart is a "have to do" because I've got so much shopping to do and it's easier to get everything in one place.	But when I get a few precious minutes to spend on me, I deserve to shop somewhere more fun.
Ego Protection	I know it's smart to shop at Wal-Mart.	When I go, I always hope I don't run into anyone I know because I don't want them to think I'm that desperate.
Secret Keeping	I don't buy Wal-Mart gift cards for kids' parties because the other kids' moms would look down on my cheapness.	I buy lots of cheap presents there, but I don't include a gift receipt when I give them.

many drew the line on image-related purchases, such as apparel, home items, and anything of badge value.

Changing a brand's image is a challenging task for any marketer. But turning around a big ship like Wal-Mart with more than 4,100 U.S. stores doesn't happen overnight. Wal-Mart knew that longer-term growth required some upgrades in store environment, merchandise, and image, so over the past several years, they tested ways to overcome some of those Half Truth barriers. Some changes are showing the markings of success, like their partnership with *Better Homes and Gardens* to enhance their design credentials and their cut-rate prices on a big selection of brand name consumer electronics. Wal-Mart's substantial commitment to sustainability and green products and their $4 prescriptions in the face of rising healthcare costs are all right on trend.

But Wal-Mart stumbled in women's apparel as they pursued their core shoppers' Half Truth desire for trendier fashions.

In an effort to appeal to women's Half Truth of fashion hopefulness, Wal-Mart inserted an eight-page ad in *Vogue*, a media misfire for their customers who read *Good Housekeeping* and *Woman's Day*, as well as a fashion faux pas since no real fashionista would believe that Wal-Mart's taste was up to runway standards.

But even as the chain fought the stereotypes and perceptions that warped their image, they never wavered from their commitment to value, which turns opinion and spending in their favor during economic stress. With the wind of store improvements at the company's back, in 2007 Wal-Mart anticipated the downturn and launched an ad campaign that saluted smart women who chose to maximize their purchasing dollars to benefit their families' lives: "Save money. Live Better."

The campaign transformed consumers' financial angst into proud accomplishment and presented Wal-Mart not as a concession but as a choice.

Half Truth:
"I don't want to look out-of-date."
Whole Truth:
"Most of the time, I just want to be comfortable."

What's ironic is that despite the fact that Wal-Mart's 2009 current monthly performance versus year ago is stellar in the current retail wasteland, marketers still lag behind consumers' improved attitudes towards the brand. In a 2009 survey by *The Hub* magazine through reveries.com, when marketers were asked about their opinion of the campaign's emotional appeal, most were unmoved and still saw Wal-Mart as just a low priced, mass behemoth. More telling was their response to a question that asked if they had shopped Wal-Mart more during the recent recession—more than 71% had never or only sporadically done so. But given the contribution of Wal-Mart to their annual sales, it's most surprising that, when asked if they had *ever* shopped alongside a consumer in the store that literally pays their salary, 32% of the readers said they never had. (Wonder how many times had they been in an Apple store or a luxury car showroom?)

One wonders if marketers are as ahead of the curve as they like to think they are, or lagging behind women and their needs for real value and low prices at retail. Our advice for marketers whose personal prejudices keep them in an ivory tower: Wake up. Love it or hate it, Wal-Mart is connecting with women and commanding more of their dollars with every month that passes. Get in a car, grab a cart, and start learning the Whole Truth of why women are shopping there. (You might even pick up a bargain!)

Now it's time for the Whole Truth about a much-loved brand called Target.

off target

In contrast to Wal-Mart, Target is the image darling, beloved by Wall Street analysts, ad agency creative directors, and the millions of women who brag "I bought it at Tar-zhay." We'd be denying our own Whole Truth if we concealed the fact that all of us at Just Ask a Woman are addicted to Target's allure. Who doesn't love their yoga pants, their cosmetic selection, and their cute home decorative stuff that you don't need but have to have?

Target's retail operation, made glossy by its provocative and iconic advertising, sparkles with the cheap chic that beckons women to their door. Where Wal-Mart might be perceived by women as a shopping chore, Target is seen as a treat, even an indulgence for a busy woman making ends meet.

Target's early designer labels like Isaac Mizrahi and Michael Graves lifted the brand beyond its price appeal and attracted the press pickup reserved for cool retailers way above Target's price range. And the labels at great prices gave the women shoppers bragging rights.

	Half Truth	Whole Truth
Ego Protection	I shop Target because it makes me feel upbeat and cool.	I actually buy mostly staples there but I like the idea that they have cool designers, even if I can't pronounce their names.
Approval Seeking	When I shop at Target, I feel like I am in a "cool" club.	But I know that the good deals are what give me bragging rights.
Secret Keeping	I never buy clothes at Wal-Mart.	But if I did, I would say they were from Target.

But along the way, Target, revered as being fashion-forward on so many fronts, started to believe their own press. Target's merchandising strategy reflected an assumption that their customer was getting cooler and cooler, so they added even more obscure, young, and

Half Truth:
"I deserve the extra vibe of Target, even if it costs a little bit more than Wal-Mart."

Whole Truth:
"Every penny counts so I can do without the Target buzz to save money."

ultra-hip designers, as if the buyers at Target had forgotten who was shopping there (a customer whose demos were nearly identical to Wal-Mart's, by the way).

The shoe department was flooded with names the average woman on a budget had never heard of, such as Miss Trish of Capri or Sigerson Morrison. Their Sonia Kashuk makeup line, a hit as the first mass makeup artist brand, got crowded out by four or five new, unknown "artists," complicating the shopping for a mascara buyer in a hurry. The apparel department parted ways with the likable and accessible Mizrahi and moved to a superyoung group of unknowns—and soon unboughts.

Unfortunately, Target's cool factor, which built the brand's success during the bullish years, backfired when the recession arrived in late 2008.

Even though their pricing is not hugely different than Wal-Mart's, suddenly Target's image made the store feel like a splurge, and worse, a waste of money. And the designers who might have been able to hold their own during flush economic times seemed "too cool for school" when things got tight.

Was Target cool or "too cool for school"?

And those brand marketers who told the reveries.com survey that they were smitten by Target's ads and proposition don't drive the quarterly numbers. Women do. Target's slogan, "Expect More, Pay Less," which worked to lift the brand through better times, spoke more to her pre-recession Half Truth than her newly pinched Whole Truth. If anything, "Expect More" was the mantra of behavior that led to keeping up with the Joneses and maxing out credit cards. (Sure, you deserved it. But at some point, the bill collector comes banging at the door!)

The Target team went back to the drawing board to create a new campaign to reposition the brand for women's leaner Whole Truth by trying to focus more on how shoppers get more for less.

The proof of shifting women's behavior was revealed in an April 2009 survey by The Gordman Group, which asked 526 shoppers, 367 of them women, about their reasons for shopping and their store preferences during the recession. Results showed that, while trendier, Target was pulling fewer customers through the doors than Wal-Mart, with 55% of customers planning to spend more of their budget with Wal-Mart and just 25% of those surveyed expecting to do the same at Target. Wal-Mart's gain was Target's loss, thanks to 80% of those surveyed acknowledging that the "current economic conditions" have influenced their choice of store.

Still, women's Half and Whole Truths are confounding. Within that survey, even as they directed their dollars to Wal-Mart, respondents indicated nearly equal numbers for why they choose a store. Thirty-five percent of consumers identified price or sale price as the factor that most influences their purchase behavior, while 39% identified style, quality, and having what they want as the primary drivers. While they may say both price and style are practically equal influences, we'd venture to say that in the end they would choose price over style and quality, based on the fact that their words belie the voice of their wallets.

This case shows that even the savviest marketers can get tangled in women's Half and Whole Truths, because, like retail, women change every day. Beware falling into the trap of your personal preferences or those of elite pundits. If "expert" voices don't include female consumers, the real experts, you can be misled.

so, what can a marketer learn from this case?

Get out of your office and into the stores where your customers shop if you want to understand what's working at the shelf. Better yet, find a way to get into your customer's closets, pantries, and glove compartments, where her promises of Good Intentions or her cover of Ego Protection cannot hide.

Be watchful that your own prejudices about retailers aren't coloring your marketing focus and innovation plans for the women who shop there. Face it, even if you think you're not paid enough, you're earning more than the average consumer who's struggling to make ends meet—by a lot! Get comfortable with the average female consumer's lifestyle even if it doesn't mimic your own. (The same is advisable if you're marketing to luxury consumers, with whom you may have the opposite challenge.)

Pick up the clues and cues that tell you her Whole Truth. We noted that women who bragged that they loved Target when Isaac Mizrahi was featured referred to him as everything from "Masserati" to "that designer guy," innocently revealing the Whole Truth that even though they tried to name-drop, they really weren't buying his clothes. Listen hard to learn what women aren't telling you.

CHAPTER EIGHT

what we're not telling you

With five Half Truths, hundreds of examples, and two big "do and don't" cases, what could we possibly have not told you? Actually, quite a bit, otherwise why would you hire us or call on us for our help?

The Whole Truth is that the more marketers get to know about women, the more questions they have. We know that by revealing all of these truths, we may hear "That's what I always thought" or "Of course that's what women think." Sometimes the most obvious findings are the truest, and they are also right under our nose, so natural and accepted that they escape detection. Our goal is not to complicate but to simplify, not to offer out-of-reach theories, but to make women's truths accessible to businesses large and small.

Yet, you may still have some questions even after getting this far in the book.

why didn't we report the sales results of all of these cases?

Marketers are justifiably infatuated with numbers (though the Whole Truth is that they know they can make numbers say anything). Sales results don't always tell the whole story, though, since even the best insights can get killed with an inventory shortage on launch or an ambush of competitive ad spending.

On top of that, last week's success is next week's failure in a marketplace that's frankly gone haywire. Writing this book in the midst of one of the most bizarre financial scenes of recent years encouraged us to take a more circumspect look at marketing cases and train our detective's eyes on women's behavior, the greater constant.

why didn't we spend more time discussing digital marketing, social media, and whatever follows Facebook and Twitter?

The cyber world changes faster than we can write. Any book out now on the subject is already old, so we decided to skip being dated. Instead, on our blog at justaskawoman.com we offer real time analysis of emerging media and new patterns of women's behavior.

Additionally, the five Half Truths are fully operational in new media. Think of the woman who says she Tweets to gain approval of her technologically active colleagues, but is only a dabbler. Or look at the composition of the social media sites that collect like-minded women who self-select, like irreverent Beta Moms or master home chefs or parent extraordinaires, who wouldn't be caught dead on a site that doesn't fluff their ego. Psychologically, women's behaviors in online networking and digital media aren't that different than in the real world; they're just more anonymous and private.

Our advice? Keep your eye on the trends with the biggest growth rate, like women's word of mouth, which now boasts at least two marketing associations, the **SOCIETY OF WORD OF MOUTH** and the **WORD OF MOUTH MARKETING ASSOCIATION**. Figuring out how to co-opt and operationalize this natural behavior of women to a brand's advantage will only grow as a marketing tactic.

Also, note that the women's blogging universe is like an uncaged lioness. Each day, another stay-at-home mom or chatty boomer launches yet another blog, adding a homegrown buzz to the giant sites like **WOWOWOW.COM**, **IVILLAGE.COM**, and others. Issues like buying mom blogger's affections with freebies and blog in-fighting among women will come with the territory. Stay tuned.

why can't i just do this myself?

You *can* do this yourself, since we gave you lots of suggestions for how to truth detect and how to untangle the Half Truths you may find in your brand's relationship with women. But all the techniques in the world can't replace what we humbly affirm: women don't tell their hidden truths to just anybody, no matter how practiced or slick.

We have earned women's respect after years of refining our approach and by never forgetting who's the real star of the marketing show. It's tempting to think that it's about us. But we know that getting to the Whole Truth comes only because we never forget it's all about her. Demonstrating that in every touchpoint of our work has been our hallmark, and as any marketer will admit, setting aside our own egos and keeping true to our own Good Intentions is often the hardest promise to keep.

but my business is different . . . what about me?

What about cause marketing, business-to-business marketing, not-for-profit marketing, or marketing to women of different cultures, women from Mars, etc.? Yes, there are dozens of marketing disciplines that merit their own examination. Perhaps we will take these on in a future book. But for now, the lessons here should provide enough analogs for figuring out what's happening in your unique situation. Again, our blog at justaskawoman.com takes on a wide array of issues each week that may be just what's on your radar.

We've found that it's easy to discard theories about women by deciding that unless the information aligns exactly with your specific problem, it's off the table. That's only a way to stay blindly in your world, while women would tell you that they have more in common than they have differences. We have seen marketers in Barcelona laugh at the same Good Intentions realities as brand managers in Chicago. We have noted business-to-business experts who've seen that their female B-to-B customer's Ego Protection is holding up the order or that her need to express her overworked Martyrdom becomes the core of the relationship with a successful salesperson. Look at the forest instead of the trees.

in summary

There's a saying that you may have heard: "It's just business, it's not personal." While there's wisdom in keeping your emotions in check at the office, this phrase is also a Half Truth as far as marketing and women are concerned. Women take the buying experience personally. They watch ads with their own lives in mind. The products they buy come into their homes and are indeed very personal. The most powerful advice we can offer is to take women personally. See your customer as your sister, your wife, your daughter, your best friend. Get out of your comfort zone that might worship statistics and data and ignore real life behavior. The art of Power Listening and detecting women's Whole Truths will take as much heart as brainpower. And taking it personally with women is good business.

Respect What You Don't Know

The biggest enemy to successful marketing with women is complacency, the "we already know that" syndrome. Given that women are such powerful consumers— way beyond their 51%–plus representation in the population—we've been asked why there aren't more serious initiatives devoted to understanding them or why conferences focused on marketing to women are attended largely by women and not men. We believe that there's a high degree of confidence among marketers, warranted or not, that they know women. Maybe they extrapolate their personal experience as enough grounding for marketing decisions. Maybe they think that women have already been "done" with one big study or program, so that they know all they need to know. Or maybe, as stated earlier in the book, marketers are victims of their own ADD, and they have already moved onto some new, bright, shiny object in terms of target, media, or trend.

Since we founded Just Ask a Woman ten years ago, women have only grown in economic clout and emotional complexity. Assuming the marketing-to-women job is done is naïve. Sharpening insights and digging deeper is the only route to staying ahead of her changing game and giving your product or brand a chance at a place on her dance card.

Let Yourself Be Uncomfortable

Marketers who stay at arm's length in an effort to preserve their dignity or stature with their customers forfeit the chance to understand women intimately. And when you let your brand get close to women, literally reading over her shoulder as she lives, she will tell you what you need to know. Women are tough judges of your interest. They respond only to those marketers whose behavior with them is consistent, authentic, and female-centric. Lip service doesn't cut it, nor do intermittent efforts at "women's programs." The good news about this is that once you have gained a woman's confidence, she will cut you a break when you falter and still spread your good word for you. The bad news is, if you toy with her she will tell more people than you will ever know.

Truth Detect Your Existing Research

You may be wondering if you've been buying Half Truths or Whole Truths and if you've been Half Listening over the years. In the world of marketing, some internal brand legends spawn other ones, leading to a pile of conjecture that may not be true, and in fact, may be hog-tieing your opportunities. We review existing research all the time to identify lurking Half Truths and raise areas where a new segmentation or insight may underlay work you've already invested in. Be sure that you aren't throwing good money after bad insights.

Renovate Your Listening Habits

Our discussion of Half Listening often hits homes with "guilty as charged" marketers. It's funny to joke about M&M overdoses and backroom shenanigans, but the truth is this is a non-listening epidemic that needs to stop. If only as a way to maximize the investment you make in research, consider whether your team is really trained in Power Listening or allowed to use focus group travel as boondogles. Sure marketers need to stay in touch with the home office while on the road, but two hours of listening to the women who pay most marketers' salaries isn't that taxing. Treat consumer listening as an art worth refining, rather than a chore to be checked off the list.

Listen to the Women Inside

We are big believers that every marketer, male or female, is responsible for knowing their customers. But we'd be wrong not to suggest that the women inside a company or on a brand team are amazing secret weapons in the battle for relevance. Too often, women inside aren't asked to add their personal experiences to the brand's intelligence reservoir. Creating an atmosphere where it's not only encouraged but also expected that women will speak up about their own experiences can help you avoid costly marketing mistakes. And to women, who sometimes shy away from adding their personal two cents at the office, get over it.

Love the One You're With

The first step to getting the Whole Truth is to learn to like your customer. This sounds simple, but so many times we see marketers who wish their "woman" were someone else. The job we are called most often to do is to help marketers understand "who is *she* really." And that may be because, as we said earlier, that the brand is tying its own ego to a customer you want to have rather than the one who loves you. While acquiring new customers or "upgrading" to higher-spending ones is a fair marketing goal, be careful that you aren't doing it at the expense of those you have. Also, you may find that you could get a better share of your existing customer's dollar by understanding her needs more deeply. Today's marketplace, with women already wielding 85% of spending, isn't about getting them to 90% (men have to buy something, after all!). The game is about taking market share and building profits. Expanding the universe of women who are like your existing customer or finding which of your customers are starting to dangle their dollars in front of a competitor is a much easier and less expensive task than courting someone new.

Finally, as we have said since we first opened our doors, start marketing *with* women, and stop marketing *to* them (a phrase so contagious, it's been copycatted). Marketing to women is over. Marketing to women means targeting them, going for their wallets and treating them as a necessary evil on your way to the bank. Marketing with women means trusting them enough to bring them into your processes early and often. Marketing with women means asking before it's a disaster check, being willing to believe that they might have a better idea than you do. And marketing with women means you return to them, again and again, to check in to see how you're doing. You're not done till they say you're done.

Start marketing *with* women,
and stop marketing
to them.

ACKNOWLEDGMENTS

We would like to thank the best marketers in the world, our best in class clients for their partnership and encouragement and for entrusting their most important and powerful consumers to us. We are grateful to the many thousands of women who shared their deepest secrets, as well as their Half and Whole Truths, with the humor, candor, and spirit that is uniquely female and extremely generous. And we especially thank our families for their support of our decade of creating a company that makes a difference, with special love to Joe Quinlan, Greg Drechsler, and Dave Chapman who are the answer to all we could ever ask.

We also thank our team members Jean Crawford and Lily Wagner whose attention, ideas, and experience have filled these pages with insight and whose spirit and support fill our company with joy.

And here we thank each other for working so hard together at something we believe in. We set out to be the most compelling interpreters of women's voices in the marketplace today. We never knew we'd have so much fun, just telling the truth.

And, on a personal note, Jen sends love to Charlotte and Max, Tracy to Hannah, and Mary Lou would like to thank Lauren, Manjeet, Ranya, Jennifer, Ira and Gail, Susan, Nancy, Amy, Sandy, and Ginny for their amazing talent and kindness.

MORE JUST ASK A WOMAN BOOKS
BY MARY LOU QUINLAN

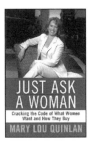

Just Ask a Woman: Cracking the Code of What Women Want and How They Buy (Wiley, 2003)

"Just when you think you know it all, Mary Lou Quinlan helps you with your thinking in a new and wonderful way. If you want to capture a larger piece of your market, read this book."

—**GORDON BETHUNE**, former chairman/CEO, Continental Airlines

"Highly readable, this book speaks cogently to practicing and aspiring marketers about tapping into the minds and pocketbooks of women."

—**STEPHEN A. GREYSER,** professor of marketing and communications emeritus, Harvard Business School

Time Off for Good Behavior: How Hardworking Women Can Take a Break and Change Their Lives (Broadway Books, 2005)

"A must-read for every high-achieving woman who's working more and enjoying it less. If you've ever wanted to step out of the rat race and start living your dreams, this book is the perfect guide."

—**CAROLE BLACK**, former president and CEO, Lifetime TV

"This book not only gives hardworking women 'permission' to slow down and ease up, but tells, with real-life examples and simple tools, how women can thrive while smelling the flowers."

—**SHEILA WELLINGTON**, professor of management, NYU/Stern School of Business, and former president, Catalyst